The Future: A Very Short Introduction

T0055132

VERY SHORT INTRODUCTIONS are for anyone wanting a stimulating and accessible way into a new subject. They are written by experts, and have been translated into more than 45 different languages.

The series began in 1995, and now covers a wide variety of topics in every discipline. The VSI library now contains over 500 volumes—a Very Short Introduction to everything from Psychology and Philosophy of Science to American History and Relativity—and continues to grow in every subject area.

Very Short Introductions available now:

Jennifer M. Gidley

THE FUTURE

A Very Short Introduction

OXFORD
UNIVERSITY PRESS

OXFORD

UNIVERSITY PRESS

Great Clarendon Street, Oxford, OX2 6DP,
United Kingdom

Oxford University Press is a department of the University of Oxford.
It furthers the University's objective of excellence in research, scholarship,
and education by publishing worldwide. Oxford is a registered trade mark of
Oxford University Press in the UK and in certain other countries

Published in the United States of America by Oxford University Press
198 Madison Avenue, New York, NY 10016, United States of America

British Library Cataloguing in Publication Data
Data available

Library of Congress Control Number: 2016954116

ISBN 978-0-19-873528-1

Printed and bound by CPI Group (UK) Ltd, Croydon, CR0 4YY

Contents

List of illustrations

Introduction

Introducing 'the future'

The future we face today is one that threatens our very existence as a species. It threatens the comfortable urban lifestyles that many of us hold dear and the habitability of the earth itself. The times we are in are critical, and the challenges we face as global citizens are complex, intractable, and planetary. The impact of climate crisis alone is pointing to frightening futures of rising seas, drowning cities, mass migration of climate refugees, drastic food shortages due to loss of arable land to drought, floods, and salination, and the mass extinction of species. Several Pacific islands have already disappeared, and in the USA, the first climate refugees are being resettled from low-lying islands to higher ground. And this is just the beginning.

Renowned theoretical physicist Stephen Hawking, Oxford philosopher Nick Bostrom, and billionaire entrepreneur and engineer Elon Musk have issued serious warnings about the potential existential threats to humanity that advances in 'artificial super-intelligence' may release. When we include the volatility unleashed by random acts of terrorism, growing economic disparity, and the global youth mental health epidemic, it may seem that this book is going to be a doomsday story. What a challenging time to write a *Very Short Introduction* to the Future.

But the trends pointing to future as time bomb are only one side of the picture.

In spite of the potential for catastrophe that current trends suggest, we are also in the best position ever to turn negative trends around through the means at our disposal. As a species, we have never been more conscious, more globally connected, or more capable of radical positive change than we are today. With the instantaneous communications available millions of people can be mobilized in an instant to act for good causes, if only the understanding, passion, and will can be engaged.

Regardless of the choices we make as a species on these challenging issues, the futures we create through our actions today will impact the entire future of humanity for thousands, if not millions of years to come. Humans have always influenced the future, as we will see when we explore the history of humanity's relationship with the future.

For thousands of years we have struggled to predict, control, manage, and understand the future. Our forebears sought advice from oracles; read the stars through astrology; debated concepts of time and future philosophically; wrote utopias and dystopias; and, in the modern scientific era, tried to predict the future by accumulating and interpreting patterns from the past to extrapolate models of the future.

But the single, predictable, fixed future that the trend modelling proposes does not actually exist. Instead, what is out there is a multitude of possible futures. What lies at the heart of this changed perception is an evolution of human consciousness. Knowing this means we have the power to imagine and create the futures that we choose, bearing in mind that some people have much greater power and influence than others, depending on life circumstances. Undoubtedly social, political, and economic structures limit some more than others. We must also distinguish between futures we can create and the futures of everyday certainties we rely on, such as the daily rising and setting of the sun, and the annual flow of seasons. We need to be aware that we use a kind of 'everyday foresight' in order to conduct our daily lives, based on certain assumptions, such as public transport being reliable, travel bookings being trustworthy, and weather forecasts being mostly right.

Until recently, social and cultural systems were built around our belief that life generally happens as expected. In the 21st century we are seeing many of our socio-cultural and ecological systems unravelling. Today's world is complex and unreliable. Tomorrow is expected to be more so. The US Department of Defense coined a new term in the 1990s: VUCA, which stands for volatile, uncertain, complex, and ambiguous. The business world has enthusiastically adopted VUCA in its leadership narrative.

As the pace of change accelerates, the word 'future' is becoming ever more ubiquitous—in the popular media, in business literature, and in educational and academic spheres. Consultants everywhere call themselves futurists. Since the turn of the 21st century, with the exponential rate of technological change, time itself seems to be speeding up, bringing 'the future' ever closer. The now popular use of the term 'future' has led to a global proliferation of government departments, corporate agencies, consultancies, and trend-spotters all claiming to be future-focused. The word 'future' itself has become trendy and trend spotting has become a fad. It is now considered obligatory for schools and universities to include in their strategic plans terms such as 'future-proofing' and 'preparing for the future'. And yet, paradoxically, short-termism thrives, in business, government, and education circles, with little evidence of engagement with the futures studies literature established over several decades.

From a personal view the future is mysterious and ever changing: sometimes it is like a rainbow with the pot of gold always out of reach. Other times it rushes at us like a tornado or drowns us in a tsunami of chaos. The future is paradoxical: it is completely open and beyond our control and yet it is the object of trillions of dollars in government expenditure aimed at controlling it. It is both the playground of science fiction, and the raw material of town planners and policy nerds. The future can be short, ephemeral, and so full of surprise that it is over the moment after it happens, or it can seem to take forever to arrive. Haunted by nightmares or pregnant with hopes and dreams, our personal futures are strangely full of shadows and joys from our past and yet can always be created anew by courageous actions in the present.

In this *Very Short Introduction* to the Future I hope to throw some light on the multiple facets that I have discovered in twenty-five years of research into the fascinating field of futures studies. I flag some of the tensions one might expect when reading about the future, most notably between scientific prediction on the one hand and ungrounded speculation on the other. I discuss whether the future is a time or a place, the history of thinking about the future over 3,000 years, and attempts to steer a course between the extremes of Malthusian doomsday catastrophes and the panorama of Cornucopian techno-optimism.

While the book will include a gloss of populist approaches, the main focus of this VSI will be to introduce the curious reader to the diverse dimensions of the fifty-year-old transdisciplinary field of futures studies that counts among its experts thousands of professors, researchers, practitioners, and students, across all continents. Futures studies operates as a global academic field, on the assumption that consciousness has increased to embrace multiple future possibilities, and that we are free agents to create worlds of our choices and participate consciously in our own evolution. Introducing readers to the art and science of this pluralistic approach to understanding the world of multiple futures is a major focus of this book.

Naming the study of the future

The English word 'future' seems to have been first used in the 14th century. The Online Etymological Dictionary places its roots in the Latin 'futura/futurus' meaning 'going to be, yet to be', from the verb *esse*: to be. It also appears in Old French as *futur*: 'future, to come' in the 13th century. However, the taken-for-granted concept of the future we have today is much older.

Study of the future is so extensive now that a panoply of terms exists to describe it, the most common being 'futures studies', 'foresight', and 'prospective'. By exploring the main terms, I hope to bring coherence into the diversity. The earliest approach to the future was called 'prophecy' and was associated with old pre-rational worldviews, dating back to the first millennium BCE. The term is rarely used today except perhaps by the media trying to trivialize futures work.

At the turn of the 20th century the term 'forecast' was commonly used to describe any kind of writing about the future. Along with the belief in progress and the seemingly unlimited developments in science and technology, forecasts by famous figures were fashionable. The success of the 1920s *To-day and To-morrow* UK book series is a case in point. Forecasting was revamped in the 1960s, and is still preferred today by those who consider their approach to be scientific. Forecasting is the closest to 'prediction' of the terms we are considering and is often linked to technological developments, as in 'technological forecasting'. While it is commonly thought that futures studies is mostly about prediction based on extrapolation from present-day trends, predictive futures is only one of several serious futures approaches.

As historian of the future Warren Wagar notes in the following quote, H. G. Wells was one of the first to call for a more formalized study of the future consequences of new technological inventions.

It is not far-fetched to fix January 24, 1902, the day of [H. G.] Wells' Royal Institution lecture, as the day when the study of the future was born.

Following the successful publication of his pioneering book *Anticipations* in 1901, Wells gave an invited lecture at the Royal Institution in London, later published as *The Discovery of the Future*. He announced that there needed to be a systematic, 'academic study of the future'. It would take another fifty years before it was taken seriously in the academic arena. In a 1932 radio broadcast Wells decried the fact that although there were thousands of professors of history, there was not a single professor of foresight in the world. For Wells, foresight was tuning in to the future consequences of our actions, as he said:

All these new things, these new inventions and new powers, come crowding along; every one is fraught with consequences, and yet it is only after something has hit us hard that we set about dealing with it.

The first to attempt an academic approach to studying the future was German professor of history and government Ossip K. Flechtheim who coined the term 'futurology' in the post-Second World War period. He viewed it as a broad human or social science: 'a system of organized knowledge concerning a particular subject'. He saw its potential as a 'projection of history into a new time dimension' with the differentiation being that, since it cannot make use of written or oral records, futurology will use methods such as interpretation, generalization, and speculation, like cultural anthropology or theoretical sociology. The term is rarely used today.

In 1957 French philosopher, businessman, and educator Gaston Berger (1896–1960) coined the term 'prospective' when he set up the Centre International de Prospective in Paris, and published the journal *Prospective*. For Berger, prospective was the mirror image of retrospective. It was not just about trying to see the future, but about taking action. The term is most commonly used today among French prospectivists such as Michel Godet and Latin American futurists such as Guillermina Baena Paz and Antonio Alonso-Concheiro. Godet reaffirms the action aspect of Berger's prospective: 'Prospective considers the future to be the result of human agency, which, in turn, is strongly conditioned by human desires, projects, and dreams.' A few years after Berger founded his centre, French prospectivist Bertrand de Jouvenel (1903–87) founded the organization Futuribles in Paris (1960), and also published a journal of the same name, still in circulation today. De Jouvenel's conviction was that the future is not predetermined, and simply unknown, but that a wide range of futures is possible for any given state of affairs, meaning that the actual outcome would be according to our intervening actions—human agency.

In parallel with these European developments, in the USA the RAND Corporation was developing the scenario planning methodology, particularly through Herman Kahn's 1960s work on post-war scenarios. French oil executive Pierre Wack was reputedly the first to work with scenarios in the private sector, working with Royal Dutch/Shell in London from the 1970s. Godet has used scenarios since the 1980s in his French prospective approach, followed by Peter Schwartz's Global Business Network scenario approach. Scenario planning is a broad methodology that can be used within any of the various approaches to futures studies. To understand which futures approach underlies the scenarios we need to look for the key terms, theories, goals, descriptors, and associated research methods.

In the late 1960s some of the big changes that were happening in other disciplines also impacted the study of the future. The most important change in the naming of the study arose with the insistence by leading thinkers in the field such as James Dator and Eleonora Masini that both the terms futures and studies needed to be plural, bringing about the birth of 'futures studies'. This move to pluralize the terms may seem minor but it reflected a deeper philosophical and political manoeuvre to democratize and pluralize the future. The pluralization of futures studies was formalized by the founding in 1973 of the World Futures Studies Federation. Futures studies as I use the term in this book is a transdisciplinary academic field combining education, philosophy, sociology, history, psychology, and economic theory with real-life observation to propose, for the benefit of society, not just one kind of future but multiple futures. Current researchers who are working from this broad stance use this plural term 'futures studies' to describe the overall field of research and practice.

Wells's term foresight made a comeback in the 1990s and is quite commonly used today especially by practitioners. The High Level Expert Group for Foresight in the European Commission describes it like this: 'Foresight can be defined as a systematic, participatory, future intelligence gathering and medium-to-long-term vision-building process...aimed at present-day decisions and mobilizing joint actions.' Strategic foresight is generally regarded as a sub-branch of foresight. Richard Slaughter describes it as a fusion of futures methods with those of strategic management. On the other hand, for those who work in the areas of strategy and planning, strategic foresight is a relatively new and often welcome extension to their work into longer-range contexts. Godet suggests strategic foresight is the closest English term to represent the French approach, except that it lacks the activism of the French prospective.

There are a few other terms that have been used in more minor ways by individuals or subgroups and I can only mention them briefly here.

The term 'prognostics' was used in Soviet Eastern Europe, during the Cold War period. Masini linked it with scientific positivism and Lenin's thought. Hungarian futurist Erzsébet Novaky explains that in prognostics the explorative aspect of futures studies was subordinated to the centralized planning of the Soviet regime. In the 1960s and 1970s some futurists working to empower participants to create alternative preferred futures used the term 'futuristics' but it never gained much traction. Another term, 'futurism', was widely used in the early 1970s to characterize the field but is generally avoided today because of its association with the far right radical art movement in Italy during the early 20th century.

The term 'anticipation', first used by Wells in his 1901 book *Anticipations*, is also making a reappearance. Notably, Wells used the plural form to imply multiplicity and openness rather than foreclosure. In the 1980s Frank Biancheri coined the term 'political anticipation' in a pan-European political context. Robert Rosen subsequently drew from Soviet anticipatory systems approaches to try to legitimize future study as a science through mathematics, computer science, and cybernetics. Recent developments include Project Anticipation at the University of Trento, Italy, and the Anticipation Research Group, Bristol University, UK.

The newest term in the futures line-up is 'trend spotting'. More often than not it refers to aggregation of past or current information, for the purpose of extrapolation. While trend spotting has a contemporary buzz to it, it is fundamentally tied to the belief that the future is nothing more than a projection of past trends. This term is popular with consultants looking to give their clients an appearance of being very current, and having a competitive edge. Ironically this lightweight populist approach that lacks the depth of scholarship of some approaches discussed may be quite commercially successful, for example in market research.

Times have changed since Wells put out his 1932 call—there are now several professors of foresight in the world. Furthermore, over the past fifty years numerous university courses have engaged in futures studies, many of them at Masters level; dozens of national institutions and several global NGOs have been founded to research and/or apply long-term thinking; multiple methodologies have been developed; hundreds of books have been published; and there are now at least five distinct philosophical approaches to futures studies.

In summary, after a century of different names for studying the future, some competing with each other for pre-eminence, there is a general consensus that there is a transdisciplinary field called futures studies. Even those people who prefer terms such as strategic foresight, scenario planning, or prospective would agree that these notions are incorporated within the complex pluralism of futures studies.

Is the future a utopian place?

Historians of the future often look to utopian literature as evidence of early future concepts. A brief discussion of utopias will throw some light on whether the future is to be thought of as a time yet to come, or an imagined place representing our fears or desires writ large. The idea of utopia as an imagined ideal place is often associated with the future. Furthermore, frightening futures, such as those frequently depicted in science fiction movies, are called dystopias. Essentially, utopias and dystopias are stories about desired and feared futures occurring in places other than the 'here and now'. But there is a more complex interwoven relationship between the concepts of utopia/dystopia, the future, place, and time.

The utopian genre as we know it today originated in ancient Greece, with Plato's *Republic* being widely regarded as the first serious attempt at creating a utopian model of civilization. More correctly it was a eu-topia—meaning a good place. This laid foundations for others to write their idealized visions of a place where life was more perfect. Paradoxically, it was at that point in ancient history, when Greek philosophers were proposing the concept of linear time (past, present, and future), that the idea of 'utopia as an imagined place' appeared—beginning with Plato's *Republic*. Lyman Tower Sargent in *Utopianism: A Very Short Introduction* distinguishes between these formal utopias that began in classical Greece and Rome, and the earlier utopian myths that harked back to a past golden age. The *Republic* was not called a utopia at the time because the term was not used until the early 1500s when Thomas More (1478–1535) wrote his book *Utopia*.

The early utopias were very much grounded in an 'other place' so their potential to influence the future (or 'other time') was implied rather than explicit. Such a utopian narrative was a parable of a better place with hidden implications for how things could be done differently in the future. An early example of a simple dystopia related to place is the myth of St George and the dragon. Whether it is based on fact or fiction it is a narrative that tells us that in those days, early in the first millennium CE, dystopias were relatively simple and binary: the village is threatened by a dragon; a courageous young man kills the dragon; the village is safe—especially the damsel in distress—and life is returned to its happy utopian simplicity.

Like all concepts the notions of utopia and dystopia have themselves evolved.

It was later, towards the end of the 18th century, that the utopian narrative took a more explicit futures-turn. Sociologist Wendell Bell explains it this way:

> At the end of the eighteenth century, a significant shift from space to time took place in utopian writing. The typical setting of the ideal society (or its opposite, dystopia) radically changed from a different place at the same time to the same place at a different time.

11

Historian of the future Ignatius F. Clarke made a similar point about the 'decline of the old-style terrestrial utopias' only to be replaced with a new focus on the 'ideal state of the future' in the literature of the technologically progressive nations. As societies became more complex, so did utopias and dystopias.

A paradox of more recent utopian futures narratives is that many utopias are constructed through a totalitarian imposition by government forces, or some form of social engineering. Most utopias have dominant ideological aspects, which in many cases border on totalitarianism. As a global society our recognition of this increased in the 20th century with the collapse of totalitarian systems, precipitating a flourishing of dystopian fiction. Another paradox is that linear models of how civilizations develop are always value-laden. Some are weighted towards an idealized future whereby the past is problematized as primitive, while progress, development, and evolution are lauded as unilinear paths to civilization. The opposite weighting is applied in theories and ideologies that demonize the present and look to a romantic past in an idealized way—they utopianize the past.

Going forward into our present-day ideas of utopia and dystopia what do they tell us about the future, time and place? Some of the science fiction movies today could be categorized within Bell's post-18th-century type (same place, different time). For example the Mad Max series is set on earth but on a future earth that has been devastated. However, many contemporary futuristic movies are set in colonies in outer space, for example the Star Trek and Star Wars series, the Alien series, the Terminator franchise. This creates a third type distinct from Bell's other two types. This third type, very common today, is set in a different time (the future) and a different place (outer space). There is also a much greater concentration of dystopian, even apocalyptic, narratives in the popular mass media today than there is utopian.

Is the future a time yet to come?

A common assumption when thinking about the future is that humans have always had a three-part idea of time—consisting of past, present, and future. This is not how humans have always viewed time and is not how all cultures view time today. This linear view of time emerged about 2,500 years ago, in parallel with the origins of Western philosophy in ancient Greece. Prior to this period we humans lived in a more embedded, cyclical sense of time governed at the cosmic scale by the large astronomical cycles, and at the everyday scale by the rhythms of the seasons and the solar and lunar cycles.

The cultural evolution literature tells us that, from the time of Plato, humans were expanding their views of the world as represented in myths, stories, epic poems, and pictographs, to more abstract, thought-out conceptions of the world. Evolution of consciousness researchers explain that the newfound ability to form abstract mental concepts enabled the Greek philosophers and mathematicians to lay the foundations for the kind of logical thought that we aspire to today. The striving of philosophers such as Parmenides and Heraclitus to understand the nature of existence led to the formation of a variety of schools of philosophical thought with respect to time. The key ideas were that time is eternal, permanent, and unchanging, versus the notion that time is the measurement of change. The latter concept led to the idea that existence can be divided into linear blocks of time: past, present, and future in contrast with the old cyclical view of time as flow. Along with the linear concept of time came philosophy and mathematics. Pictograms were replaced with alphabets and written history was born, meaning that the past was becoming more fixed, and the future was becoming conceptually distinct, and an object of interest in its own right. This linear view of time continued to dominate in the West until the turn of the 20th century.

The quest to tame time

As part of the human quest to understand and tame our world we set out thousands of years ago to measure and control time, in the hope of controlling our future. This was achieved on the macro scale through calendars and astrolabes that measured the passing of the sun, phases of the moon, and the patterns of the stars and planets. On a micro scale it was achieved through clocks. These two types of time machines—calendars and clocks—were not always as separate as they are today.

Most of the historical calendars we know about today (Persian Achaemenid, Chinese, Mayan, Roman, and Julian) were invented 2,000–3,000 years ago. This was the same era when Greek philosophers were reframing time from its cyclical to its linear shape and developing abstract thinking.

The ancient Persian culture is an interesting example of an early culture with a strong relationship to both time and the future. The old Persian calendar was a solar calendar and is one of the oldest chronological records in human history, having been in existence in the second millennium BCE, pre-dating Zoroaster. There are complete archaeological records going back to at least 330 BCE for the version known as the Achaemenid calendar (see Figure 1a), which was adopted by the Greeks after the conquest of Babylon. The Persian calendar is still regarded today as being highly precise as it is calibrated astronomically rather than mathematically. It is still the official calendar for Iran and Afghanistan.

At around the same period as the Persians, the Chinese developed a calendar based primarily on lunar cycles. While the Chinese today use the modern Gregorian calendar for civil purposes, they still use the Chinese calendar to determine their festivals, such as the Chinese New Year.

1a. *The Nabonidus Chronicle*, an ancient Babylonian text, reports that the Greeks adopted the Persian Achaemenid Calendar in 330 BCE.

The Mayan civilization also had a calendar in the first millennium BCE and it is more complex than either the Persian solar calendar or the Chinese lunar calendar. The Mayan calendar involves a complex interlacing of three different cycles of time with one of those cycles—the Great Cycle—ending on 31 December 2012. There was much media publicity about this in 2012 because of lack of understanding of the complexity of the calendar leading to misinterpretation and the claims that this spelled the end of the world. What is particularly interesting about the Mayan calendar is that it includes as its third cycle what is called the Long Count.

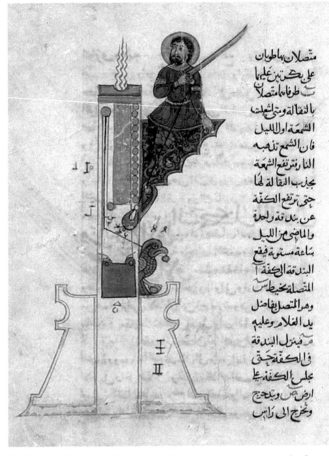

1b. Ancient Syrian candle clock, 1315 CE. From al Jazari's 'Book of Knowledge of Ingenious Mechanical Devices'.

This is where we begin to find the relevance to futures thinking and in particular the contrast between the short-termism of the dominant societal paradigm and long-range thinking, for example the 'long now' concept developed by the Long Now Foundation in San Francisco.

From the European perspective, both the Roman calendar and the Julian calendar also appeared in the first millennium BCE. The Roman calendar, based on lunar cycles like the Chinese calendar, developed around 750 BCE. The Julian calendar introduced by Julius Caesar in 45 BCE replaced the Roman calendar and is still used by some orthodox churches today. It took another 1,500 years before the Gregorian calendar, which we take for granted globally today, was introduced.

Calendars demonstrate how humans tried to understand and, up to a point, to predict the patterns of the macro-time cycles of the sun, moon, and stars, in order to get a grasp on the future.

Clocks, on the other hand, were used to measure time on a more micro-scale. Their purpose was to assist with the ordering of day-to-day activities. Before the invention of mechanical clocks in the 14th century humans devised numerous ingenious ways and means to measure the passing of time. For thousands of years we measured time with sundials and stone circles, water clocks, candle clocks (see Figure 1b), and hourglasses, before we developed the technology to invent the pendulums, springs, and gears required for mechanical clocks and watches.

In the border zone between calendars and clocks we find astrological clocks and astrolabes. The early development of clocks included astronomical/astrological features, indicating notions of time that were still connected with cosmic cycles—beautifully exemplified by the astrological clock in Prague (see Figure 2a). Note the complex aesthetics and dynamics within this integrated work of science and art that has sat for over 600 years on the town hall façade in the old town square of Prague.

Contrast this with the pared-down aesthetic of the digital smartwatch (see Figure 2b). The smartwatch, otherwise called a wearable computer, for all its high-tech sophistication, can only be worn by one individual, and cannot hope to have the cultural

2a. Prague astronomical clock, 1410 CE. Mounted on the southern wall of the Town Hall in the Old Town Square, it is the oldest astronomical clock in the world still operating.

power of an icon like the town hall clock in Prague. In spite of being able to record our voices, run mobile apps, perform basic tasks, calculations, and translations, the digital smartwatch at best gives its wearer a type of virtual connectedness. Requiring recharging every two days it is locked into short-termism and will either fail, or be superseded by a 'smarter' watch, within two years of its launch.

Both the astronomical clock in the centre of the old town in Prague and the smartwatches for sale in the airports of Beijing and Singapore 'tell the time'. But what time are we talking about? And what do these different kinds of time tell us about the future of times yet to become?

2b. **Digital Pebble smartwatch, 2016.**

While we may feel we are locked into a worrying future that we cannot escape from, learning about different ways to think about the future gives us more choice and can empower us to create alternative futures from the myriad possibilities out there.

Chapter 1
Three thousand years of futures

History of time consciousness

By understanding how humans in the past have storied and framed the future, we can gain a deeper appreciation of the significance of futures thinking. If we explore 'the past of the future' and its links with 'present-day futures' we will be better prepared to create wiser futures for tomorrow.

Our evolving views about the future, and their connection with time, are interwoven with the evolution of human consciousness. Cultural historians and consciousness researchers have provided ample evidence that Charles Darwin's biological theories are not the entire story of evolution. Theories about the evolution of culture and consciousness were already circulating in the late 18th century between German idealist and romantic philosophers such as Georg Wilhelm Friedrich Hegel, Johann Wolfgang von Goethe, and Friedrich Wilhelm Joseph Schelling. The idea that human consciousness has evolved over great time periods is central to the work of 20th-century thinkers such as Rudolf Steiner, Pierre Teilhard de Chardin, Jean Gebser, Jürgen Habermas, Marshall McLuhan, and Ken Wilber, to name a few. Evolution of consciousness has influenced how we have historically viewed time and the future.

Cultural historian Gebser distils twenty years of research across thousands of years of human consciousness in his book *The Ever-Present Origin*. He theorized that five structures of consciousness developed throughout human history, calling them archaic, magic, mythical, mental, and integral (emerging). Gebser, Steiner, and Wilber also claimed that time consciousness changed with the evolving consciousness of humans throughout history. British sociologist Barbara Adam, who writes extensively on social time and the future, draws on Gebser's detailed history of culture in her book *Time*. Sociologist of futures studies Eleonora Masini undertook an analysis of time and the future in sociological, historical, and anthropological terms. Here is a brief description of Gebser's structures including the type of time consciousness that he and others associate with it.

Archaic consciousness was experienced by the earliest of humans well before recorded history and little can be known about it. Gebser's view is that the earliest of humans lived in a kind of pre-temporal experience that he called the 'ever-present origin' or 'eternal now'. Feminist futurist Ivana Milojević refers to this earliest phase as the Dreamtime, which she also calls the eternal now.

Early hunter-gatherers, nomadic peoples, and cave dwellers, who lived very close to nature, up to and including the Ice Age, experienced what Gebser called magic consciousness. He called their temporal consciousness 'timelessness' and also claimed we can have a taste of it as modern humans when we listen to music, or have other blissful experiences. Barbara Adam uses the phrase 'a time before temporality' to refer to this ancient time when humans lived in a kind of embeddedness and unity with the whole, as in magic consciousness.

The shift from magic to mythical consciousness paralleled the shift from nomadic life to settled agricultural villages and the world's first cities. Mythical consciousness is associated with the development of language systems that enable complex mythology and pictographic writing, astronomy, and more complex social groupings. Gebser calls the time consciousness of this mythical period 'rhythmic/cyclical'. Masini agrees, referring to the cyclical time perspective found in the mythological narratives of Buddhist and Hindu cultures.

Gebser and others place the origins of mental-rational consciousness in the ancient Greek period of the great philosophers. It led to intellectual and cultural leaps through alphabetic writing, philosophy, mathematics, elite formal education, and formal legal systems. Gebser, Steiner, and Wilber all refer to the beginnings of the concept of linear time in this period, and by association, the beginnings of the default idea of the future that we have today. Masini's linear time concept also originated in the Graeco-Roman era and is symbolized by an arrow. It later came to represent progress in the modern period of scientific and technological development. She also points to the erosion of the idea that linear time is always associated with progress, in the wake of the Club of Rome *Limits to Growth Report* in the 1970s.

The fifth type of consciousness, which Gebser called integral, began to appear with the Renaissance and is gradually strengthening in individuals and culture through advances in sciences, philosophy, human rights. It parallels the development of higher modes of reasoning, identified by developmental psychologists. Gebser's integral consciousness, being the most highly evolved, is associated with the most highly evolved time consciousness. Gebser calls this 'time freedom' or 'concretion of time' in which we are capable of experiencing all the different cultural time senses, rather than being restricted to only one. Masini's most evolved time consciousness is symbolized by the spiral, which is an integration of the circle and the arrow, and draws on the work of systems scientist and consciousness researcher Ervin László.

These evolving temporalities have changed our future perceptions over thousands of years. The emerging time sense associated with integral consciousness will shape our futures consciousness tomorrow.

Prophets, sibyls, and divination

From the first millennium BCE, the major figures of cultural leadership in Judaeo-Christian and Persian cultures were called prophets. The word 'prophet' means 'forespeaker' (Greek), and 'delegate or mouthpiece of another' (Hebrew). In these times, the future was believed to be in the hands of God. The future was predestined as part of God's divine plan. The Prophets, who the people believed could hear and mediate the revelations of God, had great power attributed to them. They were deemed to be leaders of their people.

In ancient Persia, the prophet Zoroaster (Zarathustra) (c.628–c.551 BCE) was leader of his people and also founder of the Zoroastrian religion. He encapsulates the intimate relationship between leadership, prophecy, and religion/God/Spirit. Islam also took the title of prophet for its leader when it originated over a thousand years later.

In the Hebrew setting, where prophecy arose out of divination and seership, the main role of the prophets as messengers of God (Yahweh) was to announce prophecies. Their success at forespeaking depended on their ability to receive divine revelations, which was crucial for these early prophets, who also fulfilled quite integrated roles in their societies, as civil and religious leaders. From around 1000 BCE guilds of prophets formed and became active statesmen or mentors for the kings. Not all the prophets told the kings what they wanted to hear, however. Some of the later prophet orators were rebel-activists calling the king to account for his lack of moral or ethical character. One such radical reformer was the prophet Elijah, a prototype for today's critical futures thinkers who need the courage to 'speak truth to power'. The most famous Hebrew prophets were men, such as Abraham, Isaac, Jacob, and Moses. However, the Talmud names seven women, and reports that Sarah's prophetic ability was superior to that of her more famous husband, Abraham. Ironically, when Alvin Toffler published *The Futurists* (1972) his twenty-two futurists included only one woman, Margaret Mead, but he admits that the wives of several of the authors often co-authored their works, including his own wife, Heidi.

Women had a more dominant role in the future in ancient Greece where the sibyls were the oracles. Like the prophets, the sibyls were believed to have direct access to divine revelations and their oracles and predictions were treated with great respect within the culture of the time. These original Sibylline Oracles were collected and guarded in temples to be consulted in times of great crisis. Controversy surrounds these oracles, though, because in later times both the Jews and the Christians wrote similar-looking texts, which may be confused with the originals. Although the original sibyls were figures from pre-Christian, pagan times, Michelangelo immortalized five of them in the grand fresco in the Sistine Chapel (the Delphic, Cumaean, Libyan, Persian, and Erythraean Sibyls). The sibyls are often credited with being the first to predict the coming of Christ. Michelangelo painted them as the first to sense the coming of the Redeemer, linking prophecy with spiritual redemption. The call of the future in these times was a spiritual call.

While the people of the Abrahamic and other religions were heavily invested in human mediation between God and the affairs of men and kings, the Chinese were using primarily inanimate objects to interpret the universal laws and 'read the future'. As early as 1200 BCE the Chinese shamans of the Shang Dynasty were writing on oracle bones to send their messages and predictions. Much later, but guided by similar principles, the

Vikings threw their runes to divine their futures. In medieval Europe divination was still the order of the day. Tarot cards emerged in mid-15th-century France, but it was not until the 18th century—paradoxically, after the arrival of modern science—that they were used to read the future.

Between Plato and Leonardo da Vinci

The middle of the first millennium BCE saw a shift from human reliance on the gods via messages from prophets and sibyls to the beginnings of human-centred utopian visions in Greece and Rome. Sargent tells us in *Utopianism: A Very Short Introduction* that the earlier utopian classic myths looked back to a fantasy golden age in the past, whereas the Greek and Roman utopias of Plato and Virgil (70–19 BCE) referred to human-created societies.

> This branch of the utopian tradition gives people hope because it is more realistic and because it focuses on humans solving problems, such as adequate food, housing, and clothing and security, rather than relying on Nature or the gods.

Plato's *Republic* (380 BCE) addresses questions of education, the role of both women and men in society, and presents an ideal harmonious state governed by philosopher-kings. Sargent describes it as 'the closest possible approximation of the ideal society'. Sargent makes a similar point about Virgil's images of Arcadia where 'the better world became based on human activity rather than simply being a gift from the gods'. He goes further to claim that Virgil's *Fourth Eclogue* marks a shift from the past golden age to the future.

A clearer differentiation between the past and the future was being consolidated in ancient Rome. According to de Jouvenel the Roman philosopher Marcus Tullius Cicero (106–43 BCE) made an important distinction between 'facta: what is accomplished and can be taken as solid' and 'futura: what shall come into being, and is as yet "undone"'. De Jouvenel went on to argue that therefore there can be no science of the future because 'the future is not the realm of the "true or false" but the realm of the "possibles"', or what he called futuribles. While time theorists may critique de Jouvenel's concepts of facta and futura as oversimplification, they were merely starting points to more nuanced concepts in his art of conjecture.

Macrohistorians Johan Galtung and Sohail Inayatullah refer to Chinese philosopher Sīmǎ Qiān (145–90 BCE) as one of the first futurists in that he charted cycles of virtue spread over 30-, 100-, 300-, and 1,000-year time spans. Remarkably, Sīmǎ Qiān and Cicero, although writing just a few years apart, represent the two sides of that worldview shift from cyclical time to linear time.

Only a few signposts can be found in the human journey to understand the future during the so-called Dark and Middle Ages. The first to develop a utopian vision within the relatively nascent linear time concept was Christian theologian and philosopher Augustine of Hippo (354–430 CE), who wrote the *De Civitate Dei* (translated as *City of God*) in 426 CE. Augustine proposed a utopian future society based on love, drawing from the Christian teachings of his times.

Several hundred years passed before the next significant utopian visionary. In the late 12th century, Sicilian abbot and mystic Joachim of Fiore (1135–1202) developed a prophecy of three great ages on earth. He predicted the third age would begin in the year 1260 when the earth would become the scene for spiritual action. Dutch sociologist and politician Fred Polak offered important insights into the contrasting concepts of the future of Augustine and Joachim in *The Image of the Future* (1955). In Polak's view, Augustine's utopia is a platonic ideal that attempts to remake the world by raising it to a heavenly form—to spiritualize the world so that it becomes a City of God.

In Augustine's approach to the future, humans were passive in the face of a transcendent God and powerful Church. By contrast, in Joachim's third age humans are responsible for transforming the earth through their actions. Joachim's approach inspired the brotherhoods of mendicant monks in Europe and led to 'social utopism and utopian socialism'.

Ironically it was in 1260, the year that Joachim proposed for the start of his third age on earth, that English philosopher, monk, and mathematician Roger Bacon (c.1220–1292) published *Epistola de Secretis Operibus*. Roger Bacon (unlike Francis Bacon, 400 years later) is often overlooked in the literature and yet he foresaw that scientific knowledge would one day lead to the invention of the motorcar, the helicopter, and the self-propelled ship. I include an extract from Bacon's *Epistola* here cited in Clarke's *The Pattern of Expectation 1644–2001*.

> ...cars can be made so that without animals they will move with unbelievable rapidity...Also flying machines can be constructed so that a man sits in the midst of the machine revolving some engine by which artificial wings are made to beat the air like a flying bird.

Roger Bacon's scientific writing was rediscovered in the 19th century and is viewed as a forerunner to Francis Bacon's development of experimental method. His *Epistola* however falls more into the category of his alchemical writings than his scientific writings. I see it as a prototype for science fiction.

A century after Roger Bacon, North African Arab historian Ibn Khaldun (1332–1406) published *The Muqaddimah* (1377), which macrohistorians tell us included a cyclical theory of social change tracing patterns of nomadic conquest, consolidation, waste, decadence, and further conquest. Whether the future is a site of progress or decline, or merely repeated cycles, is still topical in the 21st century.

Renaissance futures

The Renaissance represented a revolution in thinking and culture that pointed to a radically different future. It spanned a long period of great artistic and literary creativity in Europe from the late 14th to the 17th centuries. Leonardo da Vinci (1452–1519) was a significant early futures' visionary who, before the end of the 15th century, produced comprehensive drawings and models of flying machines and war machines. Over ten years from 1488 he also developed a comprehensive model of an ideal city as a response to the plague that ravaged Milan. Leonardo's ideal city included infrastructure such as wide roads, fresh air vents in buildings, and underground sanitation systems to prevent the spread of disease, but the grand scale of the design was too large to be built at the time. Da Vinci was a Renaissance futurist whose visions provided prototypes for inventions that were built centuries later.

In parallel with the Renaissance, there was a great era of maritime exploration by the Spanish, Portuguese, British, French, and Dutch. These explorers ventured by sea beyond Europe across the Atlantic, the Indian Ocean, and the Pacific, claiming territory for the kings and queens. French philosopher Edgar Morin refers to this as the beginning of the 'planetary era'. This marked both the beginnings of European colonization of other parts of the world and the beginnings of globalization with the formation of the first multinationals such as the British East India Company and the Dutch East India Company at the beginning of the 1600s.

This spirit of exploration beyond the known world most likely inspired the utopian writers to imagine other lands where life could be improved through a fresh start. The utopias of this period are utopias of another place rather than a future time, which came later. The best-known utopian narrative is Thomas More's *Utopia* (1516). It was a forerunner for socialist visions in which the values of the community were more highly prized than those of the individual in society.

The prophetic writing of Nostradamus' *Les Propheties* (1555) is often left out of histories of the future, perhaps for fear it might bring ridicule to a field that many have tried to establish as a science. In sharp contrast with Nostradamus' imaginative prophecies, Nicolaus Copernicus (1473–1543) published *On the Revolution of the Heavenly Spheres* in 1543, initiating a major shift in thinking from a geocentric to a heliocentric universe, called the Copernican Revolution. Probably anticipating that the Church would view his publication as heretical he waited until just before his death to publish it. His publication is claimed to have started the scientific revolution, through what was called the 'new astronomy'.

In 1589, Spanish theologian Louis de Molina (1535–1600) entered the centuries-old theological debate on free will versus determinism in relation to the future. In his book *Concordia*, Part IV: *On Divine Foreknowledge*, de Molina came up with the notion of 'futura' which suggested that the future was neither fully determined by God nor fully free for humans, but that there were contingent and possible futures for humans that God could know, hypothetically. This debate is too complex to consider in detail, but de Molina did influence later ideas.

A century after More, Italian philosopher and Dominican monk Tommaso Campanella (1568–1639) published *La città del sole* (1602) translated as *The City of the Sun*. The story is told as a dialogue between a Grandmaster of the Knights Hospitallers and a Genoese sea-captain, his guest, who is telling the Grandmaster of the amazing city he has seen on his travels. The story begins with a physical description of a city built on a great hill and divided into seven huge circles. As the description goes on, it becomes more involved in esoteric details, which seem to draw some inspiration from Augustine's *City of God*. The pre-modern mind-set is evident in the last section where the Grandmaster gives an astrologer's view of the coming age.

> Oh, if you knew what our astrologers say of the coming age, and of our age, that has in it more history within 100 years than all the world had in 4,000 years before! of the wonderful inventions of printing and guns, and the use of the magnet, and how it all comes of Mercury, Mars, the Moon, and the Scorpion!

Medieval utopias were often linked to religious values and yet in many cases the Church persecuted the authors for their views. For example, Campanella spent twenty-seven years in prison for his heterodox views, but ironically wrote most of his work there. He fared better than More, who was executed.

The first scientific bid for the future

Throughout the 16th and 17th centuries great upheavals were taking place all over the world: the artistic renewal and inventiveness of the Renaissance; the exploration and colonization by Europeans of other lands; and the transition from the mythical and religious visions to futuristic visions inspired by modern science, heralding a shift in power from church dogma to modern scientific discovery. The scientific revolution and the Age of Enlightenment introduced the first scientific and rational bid for the future.

English scientist Francis Bacon's (1561–1626) *New Atlantis* was published in 1627, the year after his death. Bacon is often called the father of empiricism, because he developed the inductive scientific method. Bacon's vision takes a more scientific approach than earlier futuristic narratives. It marks a transition from the medieval outlook that sought happiness in the ideal, spiritualized visions of Augustine or Campanella to a worldview believing in the possibilities of modern science and human progress. His vision included idealistic views of human qualities and a state-funded research college foreshadowing the Enlightenment, from which sprang modern research universities.

Soon after Bacon's utopia René Descartes published his *Discourse on Method* (1637) in which his famous dictum 'Cogito ergo Sum (I think, therefore I am)' appeared. Descartes's arguments for the mind–body split founded what is known as Cartesian (or French) Rationalism and inspired the French Enlightenment.

The new astronomical writings of Copernicus, Johannes Kepler, and Galileo Galilei inspired the beginnings of futuristic fiction that looked beyond earth to the moon and other planets. English bishop Francis Godwin's fantasy narrative *The Man in the Moone* (published posthumously in 1638) is often considered to be one of the first works of science fiction (see Figure 3). Starting off as something of a terrestrial utopia it develops into a fantasy in which the lead character constructs a flying machine, powered by large wild swans, which are able to carry him to the moon in a matter of twelve days.

In a more pragmatic vein British scientist Robert Boyle wrote twenty-four scientific predictions, known as *Boyle's Wishlist* (1662), most of which have since been invented. In 1679 German philosopher and polymath Gottfried Wilhelm Leibniz published *The Ultimate Origin of Things* in which he put forward an evolutionary treatise that foreshadowed both the evolution of consciousness writings of the German idealists and the biological evolution theories of Darwin.

French author Bernard le Bovier de Fontenelle (1657–1757), following in the footsteps of Godwin, published *Entretiens sur la pluralité des mondes* (1686) on the possibility of life on other planets. It is surprising that he has not been claimed by transhumanists as one of their pioneers. The following year Isaac Newton published his *Principia Mathematica* (1687) marking the birth of modern science.

3. Francis Godwin's *The Man in the Moone* cover image 1768. Illustration of *The Strange Voyage and Adventures of Domingo Gonsales to the World in the Moon.*

This rapid series of developments saw modern science and Enlightenment rationality taking precedence over the rules set forth by the Church and the medieval (or Hermetic) sciences of astrology and alchemy. It was the beginning of the period of the future as determined by the rules of reason and science. The tensions between modern science and the Hermetic sciences are particularly marked in Isaac Newton, who was both the father of modern science and the last great alchemist, and Francis Bacon, both the father of empiricism and leader of the Rosicrucian movement in England.

Enlightenment futures

The 18th century was the period of the European Enlightenment when important writings were published that formed the basis of rational philosophy and theories of knowledge for the coming centuries. A few outstanding contributions had particular impact on humanity's view of the future.

Bertrand de Jouvenel draws our attention to an important contribution to futures thinking made by French mathematician and philosopher Pierre Louis Moreau de Maupertuis, who wrote about 'memory and prevision' in his published *Letters* (1752). De Jouvenal quotes Maupertuis as saying, 'the one is a retracing of the past, the other is an anticipation of the future'. Other notable contributions were the first *Encyclopedia*, coordinated by French philosopher Denis Diderot over twenty years (1751–72), followed by the *Critique of Pure Reason* (1783) by German philosopher Immanuel Kant (1724–1804). Jean-Jacques Rousseau published *The Social Contract* (1762), representing his utopian view of a society in which the common people were fully engaged in creating the rules of society—an early form of participatory democracy. French writer Louis-Sébastien Mercier published his utopian novel *L'An 2440* (1771) in which his world of 'peaceful nations, constitutional monarchs, universal education and technological advances' was an extension of Bacon's *New Atlantis*.

Clarke described Mercier as an optimist who believed that 'the combined logic of humanity and of science would inevitably lead to concord and co-operation throughout the planet'.

Scientific advances led to the launch of the first balloon in Paris in 1783, which precipitated a shift in the futures' psyche of Europe. The Montgolfier balloon event (see Figure 4a) led to a rapid increase in images about the coming advances of technology, especially images of humans taking flight in various forms (see Figure 4b). A flurry of futuristic fiction followed, inspired by this novel scientific invention that at last enabled humans to take mastery of the air: a vision for at least 700 years. In French, the new genre was called 'roman de l'avenir', in English 'the tale of futurity', and in German, 'Zukunftsroman'.

The second half of the 18th century was a time of great political and social upheaval across much of global society. The British Industrial Revolution (c.1760) was followed by the American Revolution (1765–83), and subsequently, by the French Revolution (1789–99). Each dramatically influenced the views of the future in their societies and beyond to the wider world.

Important theories arose from the middle of this century that sowed seeds for the two contrasting futures we see today: human-centred futures and technotopian futures. Publications influenced by La Mettrie's mechanistic view of human nature, the theories of human progress of Turgot, de Condorcet, and the German idealists and romantics are discussed in the chapter devoted to that struggle (Chapter 5).

The last decade of the 18th century was known in Germany as the High Romantic period, during which the German idealist and romantic philosophers were very active and inspired by the French Revolution. Goethe published *Wilhelm Meister's Apprenticeship* (1796) founding the genre of the *Bildungsroman* or philosophical evolutionary novel. Schelling published his *System*

FIGURE EXACTE   ET PROPORTIONS.

DU GLOBE   AËROSTATIQUE,

Qui, le premier,   a enlevé

des Hommes   dans les Airs.

Hauteur du Globe .... 70. pieds. │ Poids du Globe........ 1600. Liv.
Diametre................ 46. pieds.   │ Poids qu'il à enlevé 10. à 1200 Liv.
Capacité .... 60000 pieds cubes. │ La Gallerie avoit 3. pieds de largeur.

La partie superieure etoit entourée de Fleurs-de-lys; au-dessous les 12 Signes du Zodiaque.
Au milieu les Chiffres du Roi, entremêlés de Soleils.
Le bas, etoit garni de Mascarons et de Guirlandes; plusieurs Aigles à ailes éployées
paroissoient suporter en l'air cette puissante Machine.
Tous ces ornemens etoient de couleur d'or sur un beau fond bleu, ensorte que ce su-
perbe Globe paroissoit être d'or et d'azur.
La Gallerie circulaire, dans laquelle on voyoit M. le Marquis D'ARLANDES et
M. PILATRE DE ROZIER, etoit peinte en Draperies cramoisies à franges d'or.

Gran.le Notice 1786

4a. Montgolfier balloon, 1783. Illustration of the launch of the first balloon in Paris.

of Transcendental Idealism (1800), which incorporated his views on conscious evolution. These philosophers contributed a great deal to the emerging humanistic ideas of human progress, and cultural and intellectual futures. They are still very influential today in theories about futures of thinking and consciousness.

LES UTOPIES DE LA NAVIGATION
AÉRIENNE AU SIÈCLE DERNIER.

COLLECTION 476   2ème Série (Nº 2)   ROMANET&Cⁱᵉ IMP. EDIT. PARIS.

4b. French fantasy images of flight, 1900. French utopian flying machines of the previous century, exhibited as 'The Dream of Flight' in 2003–4. A wonderful flight of aerial fancy.

However, right at the end of this heady century of great scientific and technological progress, philosophical awakening, post-colonial revolutions, and a great burst of techno-utopian futuristic fiction across Europe, the first cracks in the dream of endless progress began to appear. Clarke describes the highs and lows of utopias and dystopias very eloquently in the following words.

> The tale of the future tends to be a literature of extremes...by tracing the curves of hope and fear to their logical conclusions in visions of social perfection, or in forecasts of terrible wars, or in extravagant fantasies of human power.

The dark side of progress

On the verge of the spread of the Industrial Revolution across continental Europe a publication appeared in London called *An Essay on the Principle of Population as it affects the Future Improvement of Society* (1798). It was first published anonymously but the author was soon identified as English cleric Thomas Malthus. Malthus critically questioned the optimistic utopian views of Godwin, Mercier, and de Condorcet, and the theories of progress of Turgot. Malthus was a philosophical dystopian in that he argued that so-called infinite progress and prosperity brings with it serious problems. His theory proposed that exponential population growth would lead to a dystopian future of overpopulation stripped of the resources required for human survival. Malthus became an inspiration for pessimistic groups that later became known as Malthusians.

In combination with the Industrial Revolution taking hold in Europe, Malthusian theories seemed to precipitate a surge of anxiety about the future of humanity. There was a dramatic swing in the emphasis of futuristic fiction from techno-optimism, to questions and fears about the very survival of the human race.

In the first three decades of the 19th century a new genre of apocalyptic fiction and art emerged, with the theme of the *Last Man*. English researcher Catherine Redford tells us that the first was *Le Dernier Homme* (1805) by Jean-Baptiste Cousin de Grainville. While Lord Byron and Thomas Campbell also wrote on the theme, the best known is Mary Wollstonecraft Shelley's *The Last Man* (1826). Paradoxically, just prior to the surge in last man narratives, French writer Nicolas Restif de la Bretonne published *Les Posthumes* (1802), which introduced the notion of Superman for the first time in fiction.

By the mid-19th century with the deaths of key German romantic philosophers, the romantic thread of literature in France, Germany, and England gave way to more pragmatic approaches to the future. During the 1830s to 1860s Auguste Comte, founder of sociology, developed his theories of social evolution and positivism. Wendell Bell suggests that Comte's discussion of the metapatterns of social change presages futures studies as a scholarly discipline.

Karl Marx and Friedrich Engels published *The Communist Manifesto* (1848), a political pamphlet idealizing a communist society beyond class struggle. Marx had a paradoxical and controversial take on the future in that he condemned utopians and denied his own utopian intentions. Yet, as Bell points out, his '*Manifesto* is regarded by many as one of the most influential utopian visions in human history'.

Darwin published *The Origin of Species* (1859) on his biological evolution theory. Herbert Spencer's social engineering theories in the 1870s were influenced by Comte's social evolution theories, Marxian socio-economic ideology, and Darwinian evolution. Comte and Spencer's social engineering, applying biological concepts of natural selection and survival of the fittest to sociology and politics, was gaining popularity in Europe and the USA.

Science fiction and early forecasting

By the late 19th century belief in universal human progress was reaffirmed. Spurred on by the theories of evolution, the triumph of scientific invention, and the celebration of materialism, the idea of endless change was gaining psychosocial acceptance in society. Cornucopianism emerged in response to Malthus taking its name from the cornucopia, or *horn of plenty*, a symbol of abundance and overflowing riches. Cornucopianism is unbridled optimism about the future and confidence that technology will meet all the demands of society. Lindsay Grant tells us that Cornucopians argued either that population growth is good because it will solve itself or that shortages can be made good by technology. Their theory was that the population predictions of Malthus did not adequately take into account the potential for exponential growth in scientific inventions to overcome the problems.

These philosophical ideas were being integrated into the new forms of science fiction, which began to include both utopian and dystopian narratives. The new genre, which became the dominant mode of future narrative for the next few decades, was science fiction. Some outstanding contributions were published in the 1870s, including Jules Verne's ecological utopia *Twenty Thousand Leagues under the Sea* (1870); George Tomkyns Chesney's dystopian science fiction novel *Battle of Dorking* (1871); Edward Bulwer-Lytton's *Vril: The Power of the Coming Race*. Each of these has been credited with contributing to the birth of the science fiction genre.

A few years later Edward Bellamy (1850–98) published *Looking Backwards* (1888), a visionary socialist novel; William Morris published *News from Nowhere*, in part a response to Bellamy's brand of utopian socialism. Morris was more focused on changing the quality of work to make it more useful, creative, and artistic than quantitatively reducing the number of hours of labour.

Before the end of the century H. G. Wells had published *The Time Machine*. Within a decade, Wells established himself as a significant writer of 'true science fiction', in that his writing was based on sound scientific knowledge. In addition to science fiction, more serious notions on the reorganization of society were arising, precipitating the beginnings of more formal kinds of forecasting. Wells was in the forefront of it. He launched modern social and technological forecasting which took another fifty years to become fully established.

Building on the embeddedness of futuristic fiction within the human psyche for at least a century, inspired by technological and scientific progress, and still wedded to the theories of progress, a new kind of forecasting was beginning to emerge. For twenty-five years, from 1890 right up until the declaration of war in 1914, forecasts about all manner of subjects appeared in newspapers and magazines. Dozens of books were published in Europe and the USA, most of which were full of techno-optimism. In the early 20th century pioneering, futures-oriented, education approaches were developed by Maria Montessori and Rudolf Steiner in Europe, and John Dewey in the USA to name just a few. Radically new scientific and philosophical ideas also appeared. Leading physicists such as Albert Einstein and Max Planck, and philosophers such as Alfred North Whitehead and Henri Bergson, turned the concept of linear time on its head. Their new theories of relativity, quantum mechanics, process philosophy, and multiplicity of time offer more of a sense of time freedom, which can empower us to choose our own time and our own futures.

The social Darwinism of Comte and Spencer came under attack from social scientists after they were used to rationalize many racist and ethnocentric social abuses—including slavery, colonialism, ethnocide, and the horrors of totalitarian eugenics. Early 20th-century cultural anthropologists developed powerful critiques of these models. Their critiques included claims that social engineering ideologies are ethnocentric, unilineal, and privileging progress rather than preservation.

Suddenly after the outbreak of war an explicitly dystopian turn broke through. A new generation of futurists appeared who rejected the techno-optimism of the 19th century, and began to seriously question the progress narrative. The rose-coloured utopian glasses turned to black and the genre of the dystopian novel was born, warning about the dangers that confront technological civilizations, and full of fear that humans will invent and use weapons to wipe out the human race. John Stuart Mill (1806–73) coined the word *dystopia* in the British Parliament in 1868, but the dystopian literary genre proper did not begin until the 20th century.

Gregory Claeys opens his chapter on the origins of dystopia in the *Cambridge Companion to Utopian Literature* with the subtitle 'malice in wonderland' presaging his discussion of the dystopian turn from the late 19th to mid-20th century. He claims that dystopia became the predominant expression of the utopian ideal, and he linked this to the failures of totalitarian regimes. The era of the dystopian novel encompassed visionary narratives of so-called utopias that turned into dystopias through their obsession with control. The fiction of the post-First World War period was decidedly dystopian, presenting fears and anxieties that a further great crisis was looming. Like the Last Man genre a century earlier, it reawakened fears that the final catastrophe was on its way. Notable dystopian novels of that period included Cicely Hamilton's *Lest ye Die* (1928), Aldous Huxley's *Brave New World* (1932), and H. G. Wells's *The Fate of Homo Sapiens* (1939).

After the First World War the future also became a subject of growing interest to a wider range of professions. From 1923 for almost a decade, British publishers Kegan Paul, Trench, Trubner & Co. commissioned an innovative series of small books called the *To-day and To-morrow* series. Over 100 of these concise monographs were published to describe the current status of science, technology, and/or society. Their intention was to forecast a *mostly* progressive long-range future view of the next century or so. Because this series emerged after the optimistic pre-war era, it reflected the post-war age of future anxiety. Some of the monographs expressed the controversies associated with this biological, technological, and sociological anxiety. The authors included a full spectrum of scientists, philosophers, and poets, as well as novelists, sociologists, and theologians, many of whom became well known in their own right. The first in the series was *Daedalus, or, Science and the Future* (1923) by British scientist J. B. S. Haldane. It is referred to by transhumanists as a seminal text.

War planning or peace creating?

In response to the First World War US President Herbert Hoover created a Research Committee on Social Trends in 1929, headed by William F. Ogburn. Using past statistics to chart trends and extrapolate to the future, Ogburn pioneered technology assessment, producing the first report *Recent Social Trends in the United States*. In 1928, one year prior to Hoover's initiative, the USSR began its five-year economic plans (Gosplan), which continued until the collapse of the Soviet Union in 1991. In 1933 Hitler initiated the first four-year plan for Nazi Germany, followed by the Goering Plan including control over wages, production, and working conditions.

Planning had entered the global geo-political psyche followed by the quest to find more complex ways to predict or understand the future. By 1939 when the Second World War broke out, heads of state all over the globe were making plans. After the war, national planning blossomed everywhere. Capitalists and communists alike introduced forecasting work, mostly the predictive variety, into their planning and decision-making processes, which were tightly linked with the war efforts.

Throughout the 1930s until the outbreak of the Second World War most forecasts spelled destruction and devastation in line with the themes of the dystopian novels. The simple and unidimensional notions of utopian societies came under attack in the aftermath of the Second World War during which the dangers inherent in the ideological utopianism of a Hitler became all too evident. Simple dystopian figures such as medieval dragons were replaced by more complex dystopian metaphors. These were found in the science fiction of George Orwell's *1984* (1949), Isaac Asimov's *I, Robot* (1950) series of short stories, and Ray Bradbury's *Fahrenheit 451* (1953).

The next three decades (1940s to 1960s) saw the future becoming the focus of increased state planning efforts related to military-industrial interests. Building on President Hoover's planning efforts, the RAND Corporation was founded in 1945 as a leading think-tank to assist with US war efforts. RAND produced reports on the future of military technology, strategy, operations, and the containment of communism. Financed by the US Air Force it was the foremost organization focused on developing prediction and forecasting methods for military and industrial goals. Paradoxically, the dominance of the military emphasis inadvertently provoked a counter-movement that led to the rise of alternatives focused on peace research.

Chapter 2
The future multiplied

The urge to predict the future

Some who know my work in futures studies may wonder at the singular word 'future' in the title rather than the plural form of 'futures'. Because of my enduring interest in encouraging diverse cultural groups, including young people, to envisage and create their preferred alternative futures, it was initially a challenge for me to accept the publisher's suggestion to use the singular form: future. On reflection, I took the challenge as it enables me to clarify how the concept of a singular future is inherently power-laden. It also encourages me to articulate the emergence of the concept of multiple futures in the 1960s and to explain why pluralism is important for the democratization of the future.

While in everyday language we may speak of the future as if it were singular, this has both conceptual and political implications. The pluralization of the future opens it up for envisioning and creating alternative futures to the status quo. It creates the conceptual space for an exploration of how the theory and practice of futures studies plays out in different geographical regions today and how the field is diversely represented by scholars, practitioners, and researchers, globally.

Historian Jenny Andersson places the quest to domesticate the future, and bring it under control through a general theory of prediction, within the early Cold War period and up to the 1950s and 1960s. She refers to the RAND Corporation's specialization in trying to perfect the science of prediction through developing 'a diverse range of predictive techniques, mainly based on mathematical methods and relying on the newly acquired computer power'. In the introduction to her 2015 book with Egle Rindzeviciute, *Midwives of the Future*, Andersson describes this as follows:

> RAND built an epistemic Cold War arsenal: these techniques were used to know an enemy whose future behaviour was to be revealed through forms of virtual experimentation and 'synthetic fact' in the absence of conventional knowledge.

German-American philosopher and mathematician Nicholas Rescher, who himself worked with RAND in the 1950s, published *Predicting the Future* in 1998. Rescher opened his book with the claim that 'prediction is our only cognitive pathway into the future' suggesting that the quest to predict the future was alive and well almost a decade after the Cold War ended. He describes the book as an attempt to develop a general theory of prediction, which he paraphrases as a theory of forecasting. Rescher clearly regards the terms prediction and forecasting to be synonymous, although some futurists would distinguish between them. Jorgen Randers, co-author of *Limits to Growth* with Dennis and Donella Meadows, avoids the word prediction in his recent book *A Global Forecast for the Next 40 Years: 2052*, referring to a forecast as 'an educated guess'.

Future prediction and scientific positivism

Early future research, particularly in the USA, was influenced by the scientific theory of positivism, and relied heavily on empirical methods, based on classical Newtonian physics, with its mechanistic—and thus predictable—view of human nature. Wendell Bell captures a central principle of positivism as 'the belief that science involves the idea of the unity of science, that there is, underlying the various scientific disciplines, basically one science about one real world'.

The idea of 'the one predictable future' is tied to this central tenet of scientific positivism. Another key feature of positivism is that its claims are testable and verifiable through empirical observation of reality. Empiricism is the primary method of positivism and the terms are sometimes used interchangeably. Because empiricism was regarded as the only proper way to study and know about the world in the early 20th century it is understandable that the early futurists used empirical methods to 'predict the future'. They were trying to establish the study of the future as science.

German physicist, economist, and sociologist Rolf Kreibich co-founded the Institute for Futures Studies and Technology Assessment (IZT) in Berlin with Flechtheim, and led it from 1981 to 2012. Kreibich describes the singular future approach in *All Tomorrow's Crises* as follows:

> Conceptions of the future increasingly focused on one single path, that of the scientific-technological-industrial expansion of all aspects of life. This tunnel vision of a future determined by science and technology affected agriculture, home economics, the production of goods and services, domestic security, military technology, consumption patterns, the health care system, and even leisure and culture.

The predictive-empirical approach to studying the future originated with the Research Committee on Social Trends in the USA led by Ogburn. Forecasters such as Kahn, Gordon, Helmer, and others from the RAND Corporation and the Institute for the Future extended the methods used. Futurists in the USA and

USSR prior to the 1960s and throughout the Cold War continued to develop predictive methodologies using mathematics, modelling, simulation, and gaming. Both the Americans and the Soviets used what Andersson and Rindzeviciute call the RANDian techniques 'to make the Cold War more foreseeable and therefore manageable from both sides'.

Masini refers to this group of futurists as being 'technologically-oriented [in that they] pursue futures studies based on technological processes'. Peter Moll refers to this as the conformist, extrapolative approach, which 'emphasises prognosis, planning, technological and economic forecasting'. Slaughter uses the term 'empirical/analytic' for this approach.

One of the strengths of the predictive-empirical approach is its perceived objectivity and values neutrality. Its weaknesses include narrowness in focus and lack of contextual awareness. It also implies that trends are inevitable and this can be disempowering if the trends are negative.

In *L'Art de la conjecture* (1964) (translated as *The Art of Conjecture*, 1967) de Jouvenel distinguished between what he called 'historical prediction' and 'scientific prediction'. Scientific prediction for de Jouvenel is the core business of the methods appropriate to the physical sciences: 'the progress of science and technology thus amounts to a building up of our corpus of predictions'. The systematic practice of repeating laboratory experiments and controlling variables is to establish the proofs of our hypotheses and the predictability of our theories.

De Jouvenel went on to expand on the uncertainties even within scientific prediction, claiming that even when it comes to predicting the weather, we are at a loss to make safe predictions more than about one day out. While it is fair to say that meteorological prediction has improved since the 1960s, it is also true that in the 21st century hurricanes, tsunamis, and flash floods can still catch us unprepared. When it comes to long-term climate change we know a lot about the past. Based on this we can extrapolate with reasonable confidence that continued increases in carbon emissions will increase global warming and contribute to massive climate crisis. We can also estimate the kinds of damage this might do to the environment, particularly in relation to the damage to coastal environments from rising sea levels. However, we cannot predict with certainty whether the changing climate will increase or decrease rain or drought in particular areas. Although climate change is amenable to scientific study, the complexity of it makes it impossible to predict in detail. In the absence of clear prediction, and because of the enormity of the potential harm that can be caused by unmitigated climate crisis, we need to employ the precautionary principle. The precautionary principle is defined by the European Union as follows:

> When human activities may lead to morally unacceptable harm that is scientifically plausible but uncertain, actions shall be taken to avoid or diminish that harm.

De Jouvenel contrasts his scientific prediction with his historical prediction in relation to human behaviour. With respect to future events involving the complexity of human beings, he claims we have about as much chance of success using the methods of scientific prediction as we might have with ancient methods of divination. This is because of both the complexity of humans and their socio-cultural contexts and the additional uncertainty introduced by the changes of historicity. De Jouvenel challenges Comte's 19th-century claim that political science is a special kind of 'social physics' and can therefore be predicted. In de Jouvenel's view Comte was 'confusing scientific prediction and historical prediction—two very different things'.

Rescher, writing at the time of the translation into English of de Jouvenel's book, provides a useful description of predictive methodologies used in empirical futures research in *The Future as an Object of Research* (1967). After his qualifier that there is good reason for the 1960s rejection of the scientific methods of prediction, particularly with respect to social science, Rescher lists three predictive instruments in use at the time. The first two resemble de Jouvenel's two approaches.

> Basically three items of predictive methodology are at our disposal: the extrapolation of historical experience, the utilization of analytical models, and the use of experts as forecasters.

Rescher expands briefly on the method of projection into the future of current trends and tendencies developed by Ogburn in the 1930s, claiming that everyone is well aware of both its usefulness and its drastic limitations. He argues that, in the light of rapid scientific and technological change and its social impact (this was the 1960s), the method of historical extrapolation is ineffective. This resembles de Jouvenel's historical prediction. Secondly, Rescher dismisses analytical prediction (resembling de Jouvenel's scientific prediction)—at least for complex social systems. While acknowledging that the analytical model of prediction works well for astronomy, meteorology, and even economics, Rescher is far more sceptical when it comes to 'the processes of scientific innovation, technological invention and diffusion, and the unfolding of patterns of social change'. So far the two are in agreement.

Rescher, however, proposed a third predictive method, 'the systematic (and preferably structured) utilisation of expert opinion and speculation'. He views it as being the most suitable and successful way of forecasting in the technological, scientific, and social domains. Rescher along with Olaf Helmer and Norman Dalkey invented the Delphi method of forecasting. The Delphi is the method of choice for the global projects of the Millennium Project. Jerome Glenn, Theodore Gordon, and others publish their findings annually as *The State of the Future*.

The predictive approach tries to arrive at the one and only future that empirical trends suggest, and is referred to as the probable future, in which 'trend is destiny'. The empirical-predictive approach still dominates the futures literature base, and the popular media view. The founding of the World Future Society in the USA in 1966 supported the establishment of predictive methods for broader, non-military purposes and also helped to popularize studying the future.

The urge to colonize, control, and domesticate the future through prediction and forecasting has not disappeared. It is still a powerful mode of trying to come to terms with uncertainty. Those working to develop more accurate means of prediction are attached to the idea that the future is singular and can be known scientifically, if only we can find methods that are robust enough. More novel ways to cheat future uncertainty appear in Philip Tetlock and Dan Gardner's 2015 book *Superforecasting: The Art and Science of Prediction*. The authors identify several apparently ordinary people that they call superforecasters. They discovered, through a crowd-sourced forecasting tournament process, that their superforecasters had much better success than average in the tournaments. Tetlock and Gardner admit that there is some luck involved in their approach, which, in the end, relies on probability.

Prediction, forecasting, and even superforecasting rely on there being a single future out there waiting to be predicted. Ironically, Rescher's well-argued thesis strengthens the case that, when it comes to the complexity of human affairs, our future is substantially intractable. He claims that we are effectively impotent in matters of shaping the future, because of the future's 'imperviousness to our control'.

The question we are left with here is this: 'If our lack of ability to *control the future* makes us impotent with respect to it, as Rescher claims, are there other options for us if we stop trying to control the future?' (See Box 1.)

Box 1 Arthur C. Clarke's Three Laws of Prediction

On a slightly lighter note, science fiction writer Arthur C. Clarke formulated three 'laws' of prediction:

Clarke's 1st Law: When a distinguished but elderly scientist states that something is possible, he is almost certainly right; when he states something is impossible, he is very probably wrong.

Clarke's 2nd Law: The only way of discovering the limits of the possible is to venture a little way past them into the impossible.

Clarke's 3rd Law: Any sufficiently advanced technology is indistinguishable from magic.

The crack in the future egg

What if there is not *one future* that can be colonized and controlled, but *many possible futures* that we can imagine, design, and create collaboratively? In the wake of two world wars and the Great Depression individuals committed to democratic, global futures sowed seeds for the pluralistic futures studies field. From the 1950s pioneers from systems science, sociology, peace research, journalism, theology, and media navigated futures studies away from the military-industrial complex towards more humanistic, peaceful, and egalitarian approaches.

Several significant developments occurred in quick succession. In 1954, Ludwig von Bertalanffy, Kenneth Boulding, and others founded The Society for General Systems Research at Stanford University and Robert Jungk published *Tomorrow is already Here*, a powerful critique of the US approach to what he called the colonization of the future. Polak published *The Image of the Future* (1955), which is viewed as a foundational text on imagining alternative futures, even today. Berger founded the Centre International de Prospective (1957) beginning the French activist approach to futures. Norwegian peace researcher Johan Galtung founded the Peace Research Institute (1959) in Oslo. French palaeontologist and theologian Pierre Teilhard de Chardin published *The Future of Man* (1959), an important text in the evolution of consciousness literature. Bertrand de Jouvenel and his wife Hélène founded the Association Internationale de Futuribles (1960) in Paris.

These individuals and the organizations they founded were philosophically and practically engaged in developing theories and methods of futures studies that were human-centred and differed dramatically from the state planning and RANDian predictive approaches with their primary emphasis on war scenarios.

Andersson claims in *The Great Future Debate* (2012) that by the end of the 1960s there were two movements of futures ideas competing for the future of the world itself. The empirical science of predicting (or forecasting) the future, supported by the military effort, was still dominant in North America. The more critical and sociological approach, emerging in Europe and elsewhere, was committed to making the powerful concepts and methods of futures thinking widely accessible.

Pluralism in the social sciences

Wendell Bell contrasts the positivist idea of one science to study one real world with the belief of post-positivists that 'science does not constitute a unity… Rather, science is viewed as being composed of many different "knowledges" each relative to a particular topic and community of scientists.' This idea of multiple knowledges is central to the shift in social science thinking to a pluralistic worldview.

Critiques of positivism and empiricism came from scientists, and social scientists, such as Thomas Kuhn, Karl Popper, Jürgen Habermas, and critical theorists of the Frankfurt School to name a few. By the end of the 1960s many theorists no longer considered positivism to be a plausible theory of knowledge, particularly in the social sciences. A central feature of post-positivism, broadly defined, is pluralism.

When futures studies was emerging as an academic field major changes were taking place in the way scientific research was conceived and practised. This shift within science paved the way for pluralism across the social sciences. Social scientists developed and worked with a diverse range of qualitative methods, better suited to social science research than quantitative methods.

German philosopher Habermas made important contributions to post-positivist methods. He distinguished three philosophical research interests: technical interests (through positivist methods for obtaining instrumental knowledge); practical interests (through interpretive/hermeneutic methods for obtaining practical knowledge); and emancipatory interests (through critical methods for obtaining emancipatory knowledge). Future prediction is aligned to Habermas's technical interests.

The shift to multiple futures

The 1960s and early 1970s were exciting and prolific times globally for new ideas, radical scholar activism, and hope in transformational ideas and process.

The leading edge of science had moved on from the closed-system mechanical worldview where everything is predictable, to embrace the quantum and organic worlds of open possibilities, chaos and complexity, and self-adaptive organization.

Likewise the cutting edge of futures thinking in Europe was running parallel with the shift from positivistic science to the new pluralism of the social sciences thus challenging the predictive approach. The first step was to shift from the idea of a single future to multiple possible futures.

By the late 1960s futurists held the first world conferences on futures studies. The new pluralistic philosophy was emerging largely in Europe. The pioneers of this movement focused their research efforts on 'such enemies as urban sprawl, hunger, lack of education and growing alienation'. These were the goals of the First International Future Research Conference: Mankind 2000 (Oslo, 1967) initiated by Jungk, Galtung, James Wellesley-Wesley (1926–2007), and others. As Jungk stated in the published proceedings, *Mankind 2000* (Jungk's italics):

> It is in the power of the rich nations not only to search and research, but also to define and redefine the future and to propagate their images along the lines of world communication already so biased in their favour. And this is *power*: he who has insight into the future also controls some of the present.

German historian of the future Elke Seefried explores the late 1960s shift to reconceptualize the future in plural terms in her article *Steering the Future* (2014). Her evidence comes from two documents. The first was written in 1967 by Helmer of the RAND Corporation, in which Helmer refers to 'a multitude of possible futures'. The second is the first information brochure of the Berlin Centre for Futures Research (Zentrum Berlin für Zukunftsforschung), founded in 1968, which stated: 'One begins to realise that there is a wealth of possible futures and that these possibilities can be shaped in different ways.' Seefried notes that this shift from singular to plural futures arose through what she calls 'circulating knowledge' but does not explain how this came about. Moreover, she concludes that: 'the new meta-discipline of futures research was built on the assumption that a multitude of possible futures existed, which could be estimated, forecast and manipulated.' With this conclusion, Seefried uncritically adopts Helmer's predictive-empirical view.

I want to build on Seefried's research by exploring how the circulating knowledge occurred and demonstrate that there are several approaches to multiple futures, which do not require that they be 'estimated, forecast and manipulated'.

De Jouvenel introduced the idea of plural futures with his term futuribles in 1960. He stated that: 'Futuribles...means possible futures, with an emphasis on the plural.' Jungk highlighted the fact that de Jouvenel's pioneering and creative work played a crucial role in the circulating knowledge referred to by Seefried. In his preface to the book *Mankind 2000*, proceedings from the First International Futures Conference, Oslo, 1967, Jungk made three statements that when taken together establish the Mankind 2000 Conference as a key to the pluralization of futures.

First, Jungk quoted Helmer, a Mankind 2000 participant, who reported the conference as a sign of the emergence of 'a new breed of modern-day constructive utopians, who will invent not only better futures, but the social instrumentalities of attaining them'. Secondly, Jungk makes the point that 'In the Federal Republic of Germany, where futures research had not yet existed, participants of the First International Future Research Conference [Mankind 2000] founded the...Zentrum Berlin für Zukunftsfragen.' Thirdly, Jungk referred to the founding of new journals in Europe that 'will group around the oldest and most important publication of this kind ("Analyse et Prevision") founded and headed by Bertrand de Jouvenel' whom Jungk goes on to call the dean of the futurist movement in Europe.

Finally, I discovered in a 1976 *Futuribles* article on the Futures Centre in Berlin (Zentrum Berlin für Zukunftsforschung, ZBZ) that Jungk himself was a founder of the Centre in 1968, after returning from the Conference in Oslo, having met and discussed ideas with Helmer, de Jouvenel, and other participants. Without a doubt, the Oslo meeting played a vital role in Seefried's 'circulating knowledge'.

In summary, Mankind 2000 and subsequent events that spun from it marked the birth of the post-positivist turn in futures studies: the how, when, and why 'the future' became 'a multitude of futures'. This was also the moment when Jungk, Galtung, and others initiated the discussion about creating 'a world federation' for futures studies leading to the founding of the World Futures Studies Federation (WFSF) in 1973. De Jouvenel was the Founding President of the World Futures Studies Federation (1973–4) and Galtung was its second President (1974–7). The idea of multiple possible futures evolved as futurists developed more nuanced perspectives.

Democratizing futures in civil society

Post-war historians of the future are inclined to view the forty-five-year period between the end of the Second World War and the end of the Cold War as being the most interesting and worthy of research. Seefried notes the loss of confidence in systems analysis and large-scale modelling projects from the 1970s, along with what she calls the greening of futures research after the landmark Club of Rome report *Limits to Growth* (1972). This greening involved 'an orientation towards ecology and human beings, their needs and values, rejecting a "cool" techno-scientific and "material"-based understanding of progress'.

Korean sociologist Hyeonju Son's history of Western futures studies from the 1990s seems more American- than European-influenced. He refers to the 'neoliberal view and a fragmentation of the futures field that began in the 1990s with the end of the Cold War'. Although Son acknowledges the rise of critical futures studies and small local participatory projects, he concludes that futures studies has been overcome by the neoliberal project, and dominated by a foresight approach beholden to the economic imperative. Son claims:

> The practical utility of foresight tends to marginalize futures studies
> in relation to the moral commitment confronting humankind, a
> vision of a humane future, and the future of others.

Andersson brushes off the 1990s and 2000s as being a period when futures studies became a consultancy-based practice, claiming that 'professionalisation and organisation was, in the end, more important than epistemological shape'. Andersson refers to the history of futures studies as being uncharted territory but numerous histories of futures studies have been overlooked. While Seefried describes the demise of government forecasting, and Andersson and Son bemoan the growth of neoliberal, consultancy-based foresight practice, they are all looking in a narrowly Anglo-European direction. What is missing from these histories is the rise of futures studies in global civil society and the realization that its centre of gravity had shifted.

The USA led the development of the predictive approach in the 1950s and 1960s, with Europe taking its pluralistic stand in the 1960s and 1970s. Bell claims that by the 1970s it was 'a social movement [that] encouraged the self-identification of participants as futurists'. Futurists were disseminating and exchanging new ideas, concepts, and methods through the 1980s' geographic diversification.

In Mexico, the Fundación Javier Barros Sierra was founded in 1975 as an organization exclusively devoted to futures studies. Futures conferences, courses, and projects were emerging in hot spots around the globe. For the next thirty years WFSF, often with the support of UNESCO, held conferences in such diverse places as Paris (1974), Berlin (1975), Dubrovnik (1976), Warsaw (1977), Cairo (1978), Stockholm (1982), San José, Costa Rica (1984), Honolulu (1986), Beijing (1988), Barcelona (1991), Turku (1993), Nairobi (1995), Brisbane (1997), Philippines (1999), Brasov (2001), Kure, Japan (2002), and Budapest (2005). As well as world conferences, WFSF held regional meetings and introductory futures courses in dozens of countries, including Indonesia, Mexico, the Netherlands, Switzerland, Bulgaria, Russia, Iceland, France, former Yugoslavia, Italy, Thailand, and Malaysia.

The move of the WFSF Secretariat to Australia in 1993 was an indicator of what Wendy Schultz calls the Pacific Shift. Schultz also points to new futures programmes and journals and 'the explosive growth of interest in futures practice in [Taiwan], Singapore and South Korea, in India and Thailand and Pakistan' as indicators of geographic and cultural diversification beyond the USA and Europe.

> The Pacific Shift is not only a shift towards deeper understanding of
> the hidden social and cultural determinants of our futures, but also
> a shift from the formalization of futures thinking in Europe and the
> USA to vibrant communities of futures practice throughout the
> Pacific Basin and Asia.

Continuing this commitment to diversity, WFSF partnered with the UNESCO Participation Program (2012–15) to run introductory futures programmes and workshops for disenfranchised women and young people in such diverse locations as Cairo, Penang, DR Congo, Mexico City, Haiti, and the Philippines. These programmes continue the democratic and human-centred futures tradition initiated by the Mankind 2000 founders, thus consolidating the establishment of plural futures.

From personal to global futures

When researchers or practitioners work with future images with their client groups it is important that they specify a spatial range. The range of potential spheres of interest can include personal, local, regional, national, or global/planetary futures. Personal futures work is an approach developed by North American futurist Verne Wheelwright. He describes personal futures as involving explorations of the future of one individual, and the futures that directly involve that individual and their family. Wheelwright's approach consists of building a framework of information about a person's life; exploring their plausible futures with scenarios; developing a vision of their future and strategies to achieve their vision with action plans. At the end of this process, the individual should have an overview and a vision of their life, specific plans for the next stage of life, and contingency plans to deal with changes.

Some futurists work within the scope of their local community or neighbourhood, engaging members of a school, a business, or a local council in visioning and scenario building for their locality. A good example of this work is Merrill Findlay's workshop Imagine the Future Inc., which was operating in inner suburban Melbourne in the late 1980s. Others work more from a national or regional perspective. Finland is an example of a strongly futures-oriented nation. The Finland Futures Research Centre is a university-based research institute offering Masters and Ph.D.s; the Finnish Society for Futures Studies is an association of most of the higher education institutions in Finland. There is also a Parliamentary Committee on Futures Studies within the Finnish government. In France this is called territorial futures. Extending beyond the nation-state, some futures research links with regional planning and urban studies. The WFSF Ibero-American Chapter is very active in the Latin American region. Other groups are active in Europe, South-East Asia, and so on.

The democratization of social participation through the Internet and mobile devices has created new concepts of space. These emerging future spaces include 'g/localization', which is adaptation of a product or service specifically to each locality, and 'glonacal', an integration of global, national, and local space. Language-based groups of futurists publish in their own language, the most prolific being Spanish, French, German, Hungarian, Finnish, Arabic, and Farsi. As the planet grows smaller, more futurists are taking a global, or planetary, perspective.

Multiple futures methods

There are a few simple techniques to open up thinking into the future space. These can be compared with ice-breakers in other settings. These introductory techniques are simple to use, have a relatively limited focus, are predominantly task oriented, and are not restricted to a futures orientation. They include futures time-lines, mind maps, futures wheels (a variant of mind maps), and flow-scapes.

Slaughter developed a four-step methodological approach to use in strategic foresight applications. Joseph Voros adapted this and I call it the Swinburne approach as it was developed in parallel with the Masters of Strategic Foresight course at Swinburne University in Australia, founded by Slaughter in 2000. The four steps include many of the futures methods that can be found in other collections. Useful features of this approach are that there is choice and flexibility within each major step and that the methods are integrated into a process that foresight practitioners can use in the context of a generic foresight application (see Figure 5).

Input methods are essentially about gathering information. This can be achieved through workshops, online questionnaires, and organizational interviews. Typical methods for obtaining information prior to analysis or strategy development are

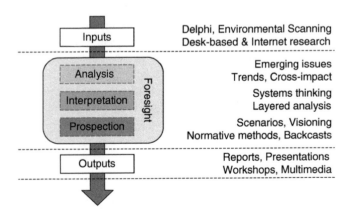

5. Futures methods as part of Generic Foresight Process.

environmental or horizon scanning, the futurescan method, the Delphi method, surveys, and technology assessment.

Analytic methods are primarily concerned with meaning-making. One of the characteristics of analysis from a futures lens is that it provides new perspectives on received wisdom by unpacking the present view of things. Analytic methods can include emerging issues analysis, trend analysis and extrapolation, cross-impact analysis, pattern recognition, discourse and text analysis, and dialogue.

Slaughter's third cluster is paradigmatic methods, which Voros calls interpretive or depth methods. Through interpretive methods we gain deeper insights into the information that has already been gathered and analysed. Interpretive methods that arise from futures research include Galtung's macrohistory and Inayatullah's causal layered analysis. Beyond futures studies we find systems thinking, hermeneutics, and mixed methods such as bricolage, which can all be used to deepen futures understanding. Wilber's integral methodological approach (integral operating system) is used in the integral futures approach. Ethnography, media critique, and study of cultural artefacts can also be incorporated into futures work.

The fourth cluster of iterative and exploratory methods is, according to Voros, aligned to prospective methods that seek to produce future images. Masini's utopian/visionary perspective aspires to 'transform the present by a *vision* of the future'. Some obvious exploratory/prospective methods include visioning (both individual and collaborative), imagination and creativity, scenario planning, and backcasting, which is reverse planning from the future vision back to the present. Prospective methods include an activism component, like Boulding's 'vision-action nexis'. In this light I include three futures methods that are often overlooked: action research, action learning, and participatory futures workshops.

Before leaving the methods discussion I want to mention the notions of wild cards and black swans that grew out of the upheavals that chaos and complexity theories introduced into prediction and forecasting. 'Wild cards' and 'black swans' are two different terms that futurists use to characterize unexpected future events that are highly improbable but would have significant effects were they to occur.

Chapter 3
The evolving scholarship of futures studies

Advancing futures scholarship

The way that the scholarship of futures studies has evolved is entwined with the history of ideas in the second half of the 20th century. Many futurists over the years came to the realization that attempting to predict the future, based on scientific positivism, was not the most productive way to approach futures studies in our complex world. Dator put it like this:

> Like many early futurists, I started out with a rather 'scientific' and 'positivistic' perspective, assuming that there was one, true future 'out there' that proper use of good data and scientifically-based models would allow me to predict. I was soon disabused of that notion for many reasons.

Galtung was one of the first to write about different kinds of futures that he referred to in 1982 as the 'probable future', relating to trend extrapolation, often bringing up fears, despair, and pessimism; 'possible futures' relating to imagination and the creation of interpretive, alternative visions including science fiction; and 'preferred futures' that relate to and include critical and normative values. Swedish futurist Åke Bjerstedt identified a fourth approach called 'prospective futures' (1982), a capacity relating to readiness to act, in spite of feared images of the probable future. Bjerstedt was most likely familiar with the French prospective approach of Berger, de Jouvenel, and others. Several futurists have developed typologies of three or four different futures approaches including Bell, Masini, Inayatullah, and Slaughter.

To my knowledge no one else has developed a systematic futures framework that integrates the philosophical foundations of social science of Habermas, with the notions of probable, possible, preferred, and prospective futures. I have integrated these diverse perspectives with more recent developments into a typology of five futures approaches. I began to develop this typology in the mid-1990s and have continued to refine and evolve it since (see Table 1). My typology begins with a single bifurcation between positivist and post-positivist, the latter expanding into a fan of alternative approaches (see Figure 6).

These approaches are not mutually exclusive, but are all suitable pathways to futures research depending on the context. Nor should this conceptualization imply a linear developmental model. Each approach represents a different underlying philosophy or theory, which parallels similar developments in other fields (see Table 1). Each of these approaches has strengths and limitations, as does the futures studies field as a whole. Furthermore, the futures studies field is continuing to evolve.

Critical futures

The critical futures approach is fundamentally about asking the hard questions. It challenges the status quo and makes inconvenient statements about why business-as-usual is not the only way. Drawing on the European critical theory approach to sociology, this approach makes value judgements about impending futures and considers the changes that might forestall an undesirable outcome. The critical social theory tradition was part of the movement to rebuild Europe in the aftermath of the

Table 1 Typology of five evolving futures approaches

Futures studies Approach	Futures types	Underlying Theories	Goals	Research methods
Positivist approach to 'the future'				
Predictive/ empirical	*Probable future*	Positivism empiricism	Extrapolation predict & control	Quantitative, forecasting surveys, trend analysis, technology assessment
Pluralism of approaches to 'multiple futures'				
Critical/ postmodern	*Preferred futures (or normative)*	Critical theory deconstruction	Normativity emancipation	Text analysis, media critique, cultural educational artefacts
Cultural/ interpretive	*Possible futures (or alternative)*	Constructivism hermeneutics	Alternative practical models 'other' futures	Imagination, creativity qualitative, dialogue, ethnographic research
Participatory/ prospective	*Prospective futures*	Action research hope theories	Empowerment transformation	Collaborative visioning, action research, activism
Integral/holistic	*Integral futures*	Integral theories	Global justice	Integral, mixed methods, transdisciplinary, complex bricolage

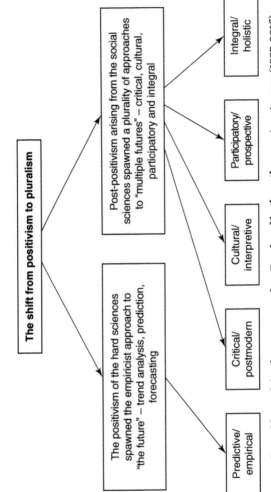

The shift from positivism to pluralism

The positivism of the hard sciences spawned the empiricist approach to "the future" – trend analysis, prediction, forecasting

Post-positivism arising from the social sciences spawned a plurality of approaches to "multiple futures" – critical, cultural, participatory and integral

Predictive/ empirical

Critical/ postmodern

Cultural/ interpretive

Participatory/ prospective

Integral/ holistic

6. Typology of five evolving futures approaches. Developed by the author over twenty years (1997–2016).

Second World War. It is aligned to Habermas's critical methods for obtaining emancipatory knowledge.

Critical futurists sought to balance the predictive approaches of many US futurists, and the dominance of their involvement in the military-industrial complex. They are unashamedly normative and refer to 'preferred (or desirable) futures'. The work of many founders and leaders of the WFSF reflects the critical futures approach. Jungk and Galtung effectively founded this approach when they set up the Mankind 2000 initiative with the view to bringing futures' concepts and methods to a wider public. Jungk summarized his view of the values that underlie critical futures thinking as follows:

> It is an international, interdisciplinary, and inter-ideological venture dedicated to the invention of desirable future conditions of life and to the design of institutions likely to ensure the survival of the human race.

Masini and Dator inserted the critical perspective into civil society. Slaughter further developed critical futures theory in doctoral research and books. Inayatullah refers to a critical futures tradition but from a poststructuralist perspective.

I use the term 'critical-postmodern' to capture all these perspectives, including what Masini calls sociologically oriented, and Slaughter calls critical/comparative. This approach is also aligned to Peter Moll's nonconformist and critical, normative approach, which 'emphasises utopian and imaginative thinking, visioning and the consideration of social and cultural dynamics'. I also place futures approaches that emphasize green or ecological futures within the critical stream, although some might treat them as a separate approach entirely. Hungarian futures researcher Éva Hideg claims that the critical approach meets the criterion of a new paradigm, 'characterised by the human point of view'. The notion of paradigms is too complex to discuss further here. A critical approach to futures can be found among Malthusians who critique the status quo and show the impending disasters that may occur if business-as-usual continues.

A strength of this approach is that it makes explicit the—often tacit—contextual and values dimensions in many taken-for-granted futures by questioning business-as-usual. A weakness is its perceived subjectivity, which can sometimes lead to excessive relativism. Relativism is where this approach most leans towards the postmodern philosophy, though postmodernism is a complex philosophy that cannot be developed in detail here.

Cultural futures

The cultural futures approach is centrally about taking a multicultural lens to futures thinking. Like critical futures it challenges the dominant global cultural model, and extends it by exploring alternative civilizational models. From a cultural futures perspective, the concept of development is delinked from industrialism, unlimited growth, and addiction to consumerism. The emergence of this approach during the 1980s marked the inclusion within futures studies of the post-colonial discourse. WFSF was committed from the outset to a truly global representation with participants from Africa, India, Latin America, Asia, and the Pacific.

The cultural futures perspective also opens up possibilities for feminist and youth futures. It is central to the dimension referred to as 'possible (or alternative) futures'. Proponents of cultural futures explore a range of cultural and civilizational models to provide examples of possible alternative futures-in-practice. The approach is aligned to Habermas's practical interests, which involve interpretive/hermeneutic methods for obtaining practical insights into diverse futures.

The cultural-interpretive tradition arose largely from the work of futures researchers such as Inayatullah and Ziauddin Sardar, who both sought to include non-Western cultures and a deeper consideration of other civilizational futures. Sardar's cultural interpretive approach is evident in his edited collection *Rescuing all our Futures* (1999). Inayatullah focuses on alternative civilizational futures, looking at South-East Asian, Islamic, and Chinese futures, as described in this quote:

> Instead of future facts…what is needed are new, culturally self-aware interpretations of the future. The goal here is to discern how other cultures create the future, what they think the future will be like. How is the future perceived in Chinese, Japanese, Indian, Islamic cosmologies?

Ashis Nandy has written about different types of utopias, drawing from a wide cultural base. Ivana Milojević is one of a handful of futurists exploring feminist perspectives. Guillermina Baena Paz and Antonio Alonso-Concheiro work from their base in Mexico to research, publish, and disseminate perspectives from the Latin American region. Slaughter acknowledges a similar category that he calls the multicultural global, while Masini refers to a globalistically oriented group of futurists who were involved in founding the Club of Rome.

Masini made a significant contribution to this approach through her work with UNESCO. She was commissioned by UNESCO to undertake research between 1991 and 1994 on cultural futures with contributions from people from all over the world but mainly from Africa, Asia, and Latin America. Masini's view of this stream of futures studies is encapsulated by her comment: 'The emphasis in this context is on "living communities of cultures" as linked to future developments.'

Strengths of this approach include its creativity and engagement with multiple perspectives. A weakness is that proposed alternatives may lack feasibility, or be overpowered by more dominant approaches.

Participatory futures

The participatory futures approach integrates the activism of the French prospective with vision-building and action research methods. In my model I call this approach participatory or prospective depending on context. It facilitates empowerment and transformation through engagement and participation. Researchers have found that being able to participate in how the future is constructed by the powers-that-be is an empowering process. This seems to be the case whether the participation is at a local level or in relation to complex global challenges, such as mitigation and adaptation to global warming. Like Berger, Bjerstedt focused on the activism aspect of prospective which he called 'readiness to act'. He linked this to personal empowerment (also called locus of control). Jungk also ran participatory futures visioning workshops in Germany and elsewhere as part of his efforts to de-colonize the future.

Sociologist and peace researcher Elise Boulding (1920–2010) encapsulated the empowerment aspect in the following quote, extracted from her 1988 paper *Image and Action in Peace-Building*:

> In the context of the theme of 'promoting positive approaches to peace'... people arrived feeling ineffective in the face of nuclear threat and disbelieving about disarmament; they departed feeling empowered to varying degrees by their own imagery.

Boulding, with her colleague Warren Ziegler, used this approach from the 1980s running visioning workshops that enabled participants to envisage more peaceful futures. Their workshop series *Imaging a World without Weapons* was inspired by Polak's imaging workshops in the immediate post-war period. Boulding and Ziegler claimed the participatory approach empowered those who took part.

Australian futurist Frank Hutchinson adapted Boulding and Ziegler's workshops for educational settings in the 1990s and has written widely about how this approach can contribute to educating beyond violent futures. I have personally used this approach with both secondary school students and marginalized youth in rural areas of Australia to help them envision and construct more positive, empowered futures for themselves. This approach was found to reduce the feelings of hopelessness in many of the young people, particularly the boys. I have also written about the value of the participatory futures approach in activating and engaging community responses to climate change mitigation.

Inayatullah uses the term 'participatory action-learning' for this work in which the participants take ownership of their own preferred futures. Slaughter uses the term activist/participatory for this approach, while Moll refers to a pragmatic emphasis that 'seeks economic social and political realisation, perhaps through participation and empowerment'.

The participatory approach is popular with young futurists who are committed to collaborative and engaging processes, rather than detached empiricist processes. Good examples include Australian/Mexican futures researcher José Ramos, who prioritizes what he calls 'action foresight', and Shermon Cruz from the Philippines who is focused on what he calls 'engaged foresight'.

The most obvious strength of this approach is that it engages participants in action research projects, empowering them to question and act on alternatives. A weakness is that if it does not also take account of relevant empirical research, it may lack legitimacy in scientific circles. It is an approach that deserves greater attention as we work as a global community to both mitigate and adapt to the massive changes associated with global warming and climate crisis.

Integral futures

The integral futures approach is potentially the broadest and deepest approach as it can integrate multiple perspectives. The concept of an integral-holistic approach has only emerged over the last decade in the literature, but this approach has an earlier history that is largely overlooked. Important forerunners of integral futures include Erich Jantsch who wrote in 1966 about integrative forecasting, which incorporated social, economic, political, technological, psychological, and anthropological dimensions in policy formation, planning, and decision-making. As early as 1968 futurists and artists John McHale and Magda Cordell McHale founded the Center for Integrative Studies at the State University of New York. They focused their futures work on integrating global trends, inter-generational shifts in thought, and the impact of new technologies on contemporary culture. John McHale collaborated with Buckminster Fuller as series editor for publications associated with Fuller's World Design Science Decade project (1965–75). In this multidisciplinary project Fuller called on the International Union of Architects to encourage architectural schools around the world 'to invest the next ten years in a continuing problem of how to make the total world's resources which [in 1961] serve only 40% serve 100% of humanity through competent design'. The McHale archives are in the Hawai'i Research Center for Futures Studies Library.

New experimental and innovative approaches that fit within the holistic and integrative strand include Belgian futurist Maya Van Leemput's use of multi-media approaches through film, video, and the arts. Other young futurists such as Stuart Candy, Jake Dunagan, and Dana Klisanin are integrating futures concepts into projects that involve gaming, design theory, and immersive experiences.

Ironically the more recent developments of a more specific integral futures approach have resulted in contested claims and debates about the integrality of approaches. There has been some lively dialogue published across three special journal issues since 2008, beginning with a special issue of the journal *Futures* edited by Slaughter, who describes integral futures as follows:

> An integral framework recognizes the complexity of systems, contexts and interconnected webs of awareness and activity…The framework incorporates a developmental perspective that recognizes individual and collective access to different structures of consciousness.

In this issue many of the articles were based on, or aligned to, the claim that integral futures is based primarily on the theories of Ken Wilber. Inayatullah responded with a second special issue in the same journal in 2010, critiquing the idea of a narrowly Wilberian approach to integral futures, and including articles offering some broader integrative theories and approaches. A third special issue on the 'integral futures controversy', edited by Slaughter, was published the following year in the *Journal of Integral Theory and Practice* linked with Wilber's Integral Institute. It is beyond the scope of this short introduction to provide detail but it makes interesting reading on the development and nuancing that is found within this most comprehensive of futures approaches (see Further reading).

The strength of any integral/holistic futures approach is in its breadth of scope. Because it is grounded in complex, integrative, and transversal theories it maximizes potential for facilitating desirable planetary futures. However, too much breadth may also be perceived as a weakness reflecting lack of depth.

Advancing futures concepts

Over the last five decades futures scholars have developed new language, concepts, and methods to articulate the breadth and depth of the futures studies field.

From the 1960s de Jouvenel created some new philosophical concepts as he developed his 'art of conjecture'. Many of de Jouvenel's concepts are quite complex, paradoxical, and require more than a passing glance to grasp. De Jouvenel's 'transferred presents' are made up of all those structural certainties that are 'structural features of the present, which our thought automatically carries forward into the future': for example, the sun will come up tomorrow, winter will be followed by spring, and the stars and planets will continue to appear to us as if they are circling the earth. By contrast, his notion of 'foreknown futures' is made up of those matters of daily life that we feel subjectively certain about. These are what de Jouvenel calls the subjective certainties. Obviously these are less certain than the structural certainties. De Jouvenel points out that there may be conflict between the transferred presents and the foreknown futures. Here is his most paradoxical claim:

> If the future is predetermined, then we can know it in advance. But if we can know it in advance, we can change it, so it's not predetermined.

James Dator developed the Manoa Method of alternative futures visioning at the Hawai'i Research Center for Futures Studies, which he founded over forty years ago. The seven-step method can be researched elsewhere. I want to focus on the fourth step, involving 'an experience in one or more of at least four alternative futures that are based upon different mixes of the trends, emerging issues, challenges and opportunities from the future, and also based upon different ideas about how the world works'. Participants are to think about the pros and cons of each scenario.

The first of Dator's four generic alternative futures is 'continued growth'. Dator describes this as the official view for most governments and other contemporary organizations. In most cases this scenario is related to economic growth, so is often referred to as continued economic growth. His second scenario is 'collapse', and is based on the common fears that many people have today that there will be societal or environmental collapse. Thirdly, Dator refers to the 'disciplined society' scenario, which is often linked with the notion of sustainability. This approach may also include 'a set of fundamental values—natural, spiritual, religious, political, or cultural [rather] than the pursuit of endless wealth and consumerism'. Dator's fourth scenario is the 'transformation society', which, as Dator presents it, is strongly linked to technological transformations, including 'robotics and artificial intelligence, genetic engineering, nanotechnology, teleportation and space settlement' just for a start. While many futurists use the four scenarios of the Manoa Method in their visioning and scenario processes, not all see the fourth scenario only from the technological perspective. Dator is probably best known for Dator's Law: 'Any useful statement about the future should at first seem ridiculous.'

Eleonora Masini is a lawyer and sociologist, born in Guatemala, and based in Rome. She has worked globally for decades articulating her philosophy of futures studies as well as applying it in some of the world's most challenging contexts. For Masini, most futures studies approaches are grounded in Western philosophical concepts—particularly those of John Locke, Leibniz, Hegel, and Kant. Masini is interested in both the philosophical and the ethical foundations. She identifies three levels of futures thinking that she associates with particular Western philosophers. The first is 'empirical futures', most popular from the end of the Second World War to the 1960s. It relies on social and economic indicators to extrapolate possible futures to arrive at what is most probable. Masini grounds this approach in the philosophy of Locke as it is based on empirical data linking it with the predictive-empirical approach. A key phrase for this approach is 'something *is* changing'. Masini's second approach is 'visionary and utopian futures' and is aligned to the philosophy of Leibniz. It is linked to the critical-postmodern approach, to desirable, or preferred, futures, and is based on the belief that 'something *must* be changed'.

Masini's third level is a synthesis of the first two, and she calls it 'project building'. In this approach people can create a futures-oriented project guided by their utopian visions of desirable futures, taking into account the conditions of the present and past trends that may influence the outcome. In Masini's project approach, the possible and probable futures emerge into the desirable (related to Kant's 'the ideal' and Hegel's 'the infinite') and create a synergy of all three. The key phrase is 'something *can* be changed'. It is in project building that futurists are involved in political and ethical positions that lead to action and through which they can take responsibility. This is where human agency appears and where Masini most aligns herself with the French prospectivist approach that contains within it the link between science and action. This approach appears to be an integration of the participatory-prospective and integral approaches.

British/Australian futurist Richard Slaughter has contributed much to the conceptualization and articulation of futures studies, particularly since the 1990s. Like Masini, one of his approaches is to take a layered view of futures work. Slaughter's four layers include 'pop futurism', which is superficial, media-friendly, and involves a trivialization of the future. His second layer is 'problem-oriented work'. This more serious futures work focuses on the ways that organizations and societies could, or should, respond to future challenges. His third layer is 'critical futures', which goes deeper than pop futurism or problem-oriented work. Slaughter's critical futures approach involves the deconstruction and reconstruction of social and cultural life, in the interests of understanding the underlying worldviews that may need to be addressed. He called his fourth and deepest layer 'epistemological futures'. At this level the more substantial philosophical and sociological futures work is undertaken, and may involve the deep study of time and cosmology. Slaughter's 1990s layered typology was used as a basis for Inayatullah's layered methodology, which he calls causal layered analysis. Slaughter refers to futures studies as a meta-discipline:

> 'Meta-' because of the way it integrates material, data, ideas, tools, etc. from a wide variety of sources; and 'discipline' because when done well it clearly supports disciplined enquiry into the constitution of human futures.

Slaughter was also instrumental in an important consolidation of the language and concepts of futures studies in the mid-1990s. He recognized a need to begin to cohere the growing body of futures literature and to create a series of edited books *The Knowledge Base of Futures Studies*. Cautioning readers to not fall into the trap of seeing this as a codification of the field, Slaughter pulled together, over several years, contributions from dozens of futures scholars and practitioners, globally. Slaughter highlighted important elements in the first three volumes as being language, concepts, and metaphors; theories, ideas, and images; literature; organizations, networks, and practitioners; methodologies and tools; and social movements and innovations.

Futures of time consciousness

Along with philosophers and sociologists, futurists have made important contributions to advancing our ideas about the complex relationship between time and futures. Elise Boulding developed the concept of a '200-year present'. This concept involves thinking about the time span of the present as beginning 100 years ago, so that people born then would be 100 years old today. At the other end of Boulding's 200-year present is 100 years from now, when babies being born today will be 100 years old. In this view, we stand in the middle of a 200-year present with our grandparents stretched behind us and our grandchildren stretched ahead of us.

This perspective tends to link us more strongly with the long-term consequences of our actions today. And as Boulding reminds us: 'This present is a continuously moving moment, always reaching out 100 years in either direction from the day we are in.'

A much more extended time frame is the concept of the 'long now' that has been embedded in an organization called the Long Now Foundation, co-founded by Stewart Brand. The aim is to offer an institutional counterpoint to short-termism, to encourage long-term thinking, and to cultivate thinking and responsibility about a very long-term framework of 10,000 years. To fulfil this ambitious project the Long Now Foundation is in the process of building a 10,000-year clock (see Figure 7). The prototype held in the London Museum has been ticking since 31 December 1999. 'The six dials represent the year, century, horizons, sun position, lunar phase, and the stars of the night sky.'

Galtung developed the idea of macrohistory with Inayatullah in relation to futures studies as a way of focusing on big patterns of change over long historical time periods to assist with understanding the present and possible futures. The idea of big history, pioneered by historian David Christian in 1989, is a neighbour to macrohistory. Christian was inspired by the Annales School of French historians who sought to write an *histoire totale* that avoided the siloism of separating economic, political, social, and other forms of history. Big history contextualizes human life and culture within the cosmological time scales, from the big bang to the present. Voros is building conceptual bridges between big history and futures studies.

Gebser's concept of 'concretion of time' characterizes how time is experienced by the emerging integral consciousness of the present era. Integral consciousness, as understood by Gebser, does not place mythical-cyclical and modern linear time constructions in opposition to each other, as both modern and traditional approaches do. Instead, Gebser's concretion of time involves an

7. Long Now clock: Model of the 10,000-year clock of the Long Now Foundation first operational in 1999. It is on loan to the Science Museum of London.

intensification of consciousness that enables us to reintegrate all of the structures of consciousness—including their different ways of experiencing time—in the same fully conscious moment. Gebser claimed that Picasso's facial portraits are evolved attempts to show this visually in that he painted the same face at different moments in the one portrait.

Gebser helps us to understand concretion of time using two additional related terms. 'Latency'—meaning what is concealed—is for Gebser the 'demonstrable presence of the future'. It includes everything that is not yet manifest. Gebser's concept of 'presentation' integrates the presence of the past as well as the future. Gebser claims that capacity to experience the latency of the future leads to time freedom, or being 'freed from time and thus free for the spiritual'. Needless to say these philosophical concepts, related to new concepts and relationships between time and futures, deserve the attention of another book.

Futures education and scholarship

There are now hundreds of organizations around the world that are attempting to come to terms with how to better prepare for the uncertain and complex futures we can expect of the 21st century. Futures education assists this process.

From 1966 futures courses were initiated in the USA by Alvin Toffler at the New School for Social Research in New York, followed by James Dator at Virginia Tech and Wendell Bell at Yale University. Over the next ten years, university courses and research centres sprang up, beginning a more scholarly stage of futures studies. The Hawai'i Research Center for Futures Studies was established in 1971. By 1973 Maria Koszegi Kalas and Erzsébet Gidai were undertaking research in Hungary in association with the already existing Futures Research Committee at the Hungarian Academy of Sciences. The following year the University of Houston-Clear Lake in Texas offered Master's Programs in Futures Studies (1974).

In 1975 Galtung founded the Inter University Centre in Dubrovnic. The idea was to create a university centre that would collect faculty and students from the Eastern and Western parts of Europe, and possibly the world, based on academic freedom. Annual futures studies courses were run there in connection with the World Futures Studies Federation, with participation from many of its members, including Masini and Bart van Steenbergen. The Centre was closed in 1990 as a result of war. By 1976 the world had its first Professor of Futures Studies, Eleonora Masini, in the Faculty of Social Sciences, Gregorian University, Rome. In 1980 Pentti Malaska founded the Finnish Society for Futures Studies, followed by the Finland Futures Research Centre in 1992. In 1989 Erzsébet Nováky became Head of the Department of Futures Studies at Corvinus University of Budapest.

From the mid-1990s futures courses started in Australia and the Asia-Pacific region. The Southern Cross University hosted the first online Masters Course in Futures Studies in the world, founded by Paul Wildman in 1995. Swinburne University followed in 2000 with a Masters in Strategic Foresight, with several other futures courses developing in Australia since then, some of them short-lived. From 2002 the Graduate Institute of Futures Studies, Tamkang University in Taiwan, has offered a Master of Education with an emphasis on Futures Studies. In 2002 a Masters Course was also founded at the Universidad Externo de Colombia in Bogotá, offering a specialization in foresight and strategy.

In addition to full Masters degree courses there are numerous other universities and colleges worldwide that offer undergraduate courses or short courses in futures studies and foresight. A new WFSF-endorsed introduction to futures studies was launched in Tehran in 2015, just prior to the lifting of the US sanctions. These developments point to the continued growth and diversification of futures education.

Chapter 4
Crystal balls, flying cars, and robots

Futuristic trivia and misunderstandings

In spite of the substantial body of futures literature with its conceptual and methodological innovation and engagement with real world issues, misconceptions abound in academic, professional, and policy circles. The term 'future' is increasingly used in these circles without reference to the published futures studies material. As a consequence, futures literature is under-appreciated, while decision-makers and policy-makers work largely in the dark. Why is this so?

First, because of the transdisciplinary nature of futures writing, it does not easily find a home in discipline-based academic journals. Secondly, some futurists ideologize futures concepts and methods as if foresight was the next new grand theory that would save the world. This contributes to academic siloism, rather than knowledge exchange and circulation. A third challenge is that futures/foresight journals are the most likely to accept futures/foresight articles, increasing the likelihood of futures literature becoming cut off from other academic discourse. My concern is that if futures research becomes too isolated within its own domain, the field may not remain up to date with other leading-edge discourses. Furthermore, other fields will continue to miss out on the futures resources available. It is vital in these complex and challenging times, for both futures studies and the wider world, that the corpus of futures literature is widely accessible. Kreibich sounds a warning in *All Tomorrow's Crises*:

> If we ignore this scientific knowledge in shaping the future, there is a high probability that it will lead to fatal consequences—up to and including the self-destruction of humankind.

These problems are exacerbated because the futures studies field, when it is covered in the media, is frequently misrepresented. At one end of the spectrum is the misbelief that the futures studies field is solely about prediction and forecasting based on extrapolation from present-day trends. At the other end of the spectrum is the idea that the future is inherently unknowable, and therefore futures studies can be nothing more than ungrounded speculation. While there are many futurists who rely on predictive methods and some pop futurists who engage in poorly researched speculative fantasy, these extreme views do not reflect the breadth of the field.

No matter how many scholarly books are written about futures studies, or how many university courses provide education in futures concepts, theories, and methods, the media frequently trivializes the field. The most common trivialization is futurists being dismissed as crystal ball gazers. The second trivialization is that futurists are all involved in high-tech, especially flying machines or space-tech, and science fiction. Thirdly, there is the idea that futures studies is dominantly involved with robotics, drones, and artificial intelligence.

The strange case of the crystal ball

I was interviewed a few years ago by journalists from two Australian magazines, because I had become President of the World Futures Studies Federation. Given that both magazines claimed to be writing balanced and informed articles about futures studies, and in fact they both did, I was astounded to discover that both used the visual metaphor of the crystal ball to illustrate their articles. Even more surprising is that researchers from one of the Grand Écoles in Paris held an event in 2016 on the histories of prediction using a crystal ball image to advertise it.

This strange case of the crystal ball appearing so often to represent futures thinking makes me wonder if there is something very deep in the human psyche, a kind of collective memory of when humans used divination and talismans to get a handle on the future. This cultural memory goes back as far as the ancient Druids, yet still inspires us today, even if unconsciously.

Another possible explanation is that the futures studies field is so hard to grasp from the outside that the media resort to trivialization as a defence mechanism. One interviewer even asked me how my 'pot of rabbit entrails' was going on the stove. I proceeded to offer him some insight into the complexity of ways to approach the future that are more recent than the sibylline oracles.

I hope by the end of this book that you will have a broader view of the complexities of non-trivial futures and think again next time you see a crystal ball being used to illustrate an article on the future.

A seven-century fascination with flying

Since at least the 13th century, visions of the future have included inventions through which humans could take to the air. Roger Bacon's 1260 vision included a description of what resembles today's helicopter. In the late 1400s Leonardo da Vinci sketched the helicopter. Francis Godwin's 1638 journey to the moon involved being carried off by a flock of wild swans. The Montgolfier balloon event in 1783 sparked a panoply of visions of imaginary flying machines. Through all these iterations it took 700 years for Bacon's vision to become a reality in the 20th century. Strangely the latest in high-tech flying machines are miniature *nano copters* that can fit into the palm of your hand. Flying either autonomously or by remote control, they can be equipped with cameras to spy into the smallest places. I doubt if Bacon or Da Vinci would have imagined this.

A typical futuristic image in the 1900s in both Europe and the USA was the personal flying machine. A series of futuristic postcards were produced in France in 1900 to depict techno-utopian images of life in the year 2000. A surprising number showed humans flying about fulfilling their daily duties (see Figures 8 and 9). So far their realization has eluded us.

Slovakian company Aeromobil has designed and patented a flying car for private use that they expect will be available in 2017, with a price tag of around $200,000 (see Figure 10). I have no doubt that some people will own personal flying cars in the relatively near-term future. I do wonder about their relevance for the majority of people on earth. The price tag will be unattainable for all but the super-rich given that the 2014 median global annual per-capita household income was $2,920 (Gallup Metrics). If we keep in mind that the median per-capita annual income in the top

8. *Flying Firemen* by Jean-Marc Côté, 1899. An illustration of aerial firemen from a French exhibition called 'Visions of the Year 2000' (1900).

9. *Futuristic Flying Car*, c.1900, imagined in the 1900s. Painting by Harry Grant Dart.

10. A flying car (2015) proposed for launch in 2017 from Slovakian Company Aeromobil.

ten wealthiest populations is more than fifty times the income in the ten poorest populations, I doubt that we will see many of these flying cars in sub-Saharan Africa any time soon. What I find interesting is the resemblance between the 1900s image (see Figure 9) and that of today (Figure 10).

The robot challenge

The word robot was first used in the context of humanoid machine intelligence in 1921 by Czech playwright Karel Čapek in his play *R.U.R. (Rossum's Universal Robots)*. The play involves a factory that builds artificial people to be servants for humans. Since that time robots have become somewhat ubiquitous in futuristic trivia. By the late 1920s commercial companies such as Westinghouse had seized the opportunity to capture the futuristic imagination of householders by marketing the Mechanical Wonder Robot: Televox (see Figure 11).

In 1942 Isaac Asimov published the first in his series of short stories collected into the book *I, Robot*. In the series, Asimov

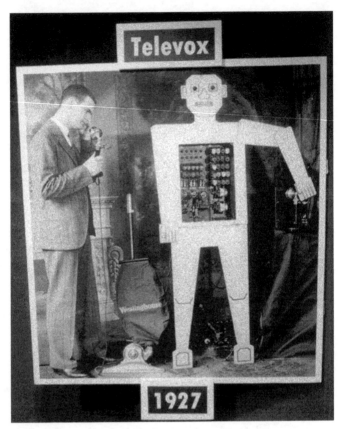

11. Herbert Televox, 1927. Westinghouse Electric & Manufacturing Co.'s first robot, built in 1927 by Roy Wensley.

invented the Three Laws of Robots (Box 2). These laws, albeit part of a science fiction series, managed to convince us that robots and the whole territory of Artificial Intelligence (AI) would not be harmful to humans providing we build these laws into them. In the light of developments in robotics and AI in recent years, it seems that this view was rather naïve.

Box 2 Isaac Asimov's three laws of robots

1. A robot may not injure a human being or, through inaction, allow a human being to come to harm.

2. A robot must obey any orders given to it by human beings, except where such orders would conflict with the First Law.

3. A robot must protect its own existence as long as such protection does not conflict with the First or Second Law.

So where are we at with robotics today and what are our future prospects?

Bearing some similarities to the politics behind the early futures work in the USA, the science of robotics is heavily funded and supported by the US military-industrial complex to create war machines. Researchers Braden Allenby and Daniel Sarewitz tell us in *The Techno-Human Condition* (2011) that the USA had no military robots in 2002, but by the end of 2008 it had 12,000.

A looming risk is in the form of what the UN calls 'Lethal autonomous robotics (LARS)' which are 'weapon systems that, once activated, can select and engage targets without further human intervention'. At the UN Convention on Certain Conventional Weapons (CCW) in Geneva in 2014, the UN called for national moratoria on the 'testing, production, assembly, transfer, acquisition, deployment and use' of these lethal autonomous machines of war. Meanwhile, the *Financial Times* reported in February 2016 that the US Department of Defense gearing up to outperform China and Russia in high-tech warfare. Its latest move is to set up offices in Silicon Valley and Boston to liaise with private tech companies to increase its arsenal of robotics and autonomous vehicles.

In order to encourage and accelerate the development of robotics, the Defense Advanced Research Projects Agency (DARPA) created the DARPA Challenge—a competition for robots. According to its website, DARPA's mission is 'creating breakthrough technologies for national security'. DARPA priorities are captured in their motto for the Robotics Challenge Workshop: 'From better robots to better futures.' This is a narrow vision of better futures for much of the world. So far the most successful robots have been produced by Boston Dynamics, which has helped build robots for the US Navy, Army, and Marines. The mission of Boston Dynamics is 'to build the most advanced robots on Earth, with remarkable mobility, agility, dexterity and speed'. The 2013 DARPA Challenge was won by Boston Dynamics' premium robot, Atlas (see Figure 12). Just prior to the event, Google acquired the company. With Google resources at its disposal, Boston Dynamics went on to win the 2015 DARPA Challenge, with the new, smarter, Atlas unplugged, which operates on wireless technology. Google's relationship with Boston Dynamics appears short-lived as they are trying to sell it at the time of writing this book. In case Atlas does not leave us feeling safe enough from the existential threats surrounding us, NASA has created Valkyrie, which it calls the Super Hero Robot.

This highly resourced competition leaves me with many questions. I wonder how robots will help us to deal with the world's most intractable global challenges, such as food and water security and climate crisis; resource depletion and economic disparity; conflicts and terrorism; and lack of education in many parts of the world? And why do many of them look like Terminator and not Gandhi or Mother Teresa?

Swedish philosopher Nick Bostrom tells us that by 2010 the world's estimated population of robots had exceeded 10 million. A current projection from the International Federation of Robotics (IFR) is that by 2018 global sales of privately used service robots will increase to around 35 million. Another interesting statistic from the IFR is that 70 per cent of global

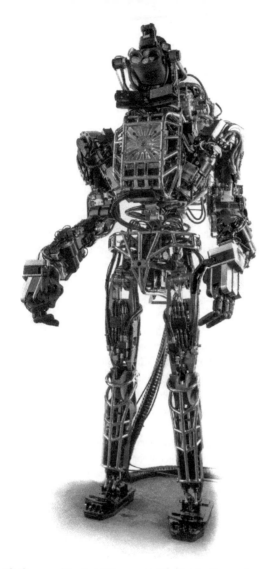

12. The humanoid robot Atlas, created by Boston Dynamics, was winner of the DARPA Challenge in 2013. Google owned Boston Dynamics at that time.

robots sales in 2014 went to just five countries: China, Japan, the United States, the Republic of Korea, and Germany. One can only speculate on the uses for which these robots are being engaged.

The lost human in transhumanism

An even bigger challenge than the sheer numbers of robots being produced is the ambitions of some developers to bridge the human–machine divide: by enhancing human capacity with technology or trying to make machines smarter than humans.

Transhumanism in the popular sense today is inextricably linked with technological enhancement or extensions of human capacities through technology. This is a technological appropriation of the original idea of transhumanism, which began as a philosophical concept grounded in the evolutionary humanism of Teilhard de Chardin, Julian Huxley, and others in the mid-20th century.

In 1998 Bostrom co-founded the World Transhumanist Association with David Pearce. Bostrom's interest was to create a broad-ranging platform for the various schools of thought within transhumanism and to raise awareness in both the academic arena and among the wider public about the potential benefits and risks of technological enhancement. He defined it as follows:

> Transhumanism ... promotes an interdisciplinary approach to understanding and evaluating the opportunities for enhancing the human condition and the human organism opened up by the advancement of technology.

In 2005, the Oxford Martin School at the University of Oxford founded The Future of Humanity Institute appointing Bostrom as Chair. While its original focus was quite strongly on human, and specifically cognitive, enhancement through advancing technologies, more recently the Institute has intensified its focus on existential risk, ethics, altruism, and the big questions for the future of humanity. Bostrom has published both a history of transhumanist thought and a set of transhumanist values. He notes that while secular humanism was also concerned with human progress and improvement, its means of achieving this was through education and cultural refinement. By contrast, transhumanism, according to Bostrom, involves 'direct application of medicine and technology to overcome some of our basic biological limits'. It is concerned with both existing technologies, such as genetic engineering and information technologies, as well as those that are still being invented, such as molecular nanotechnology and artificial intelligence. The propositions put forward by techno-transhumanists are based on an ideology of technological determinism, meaning that the development of a society and its cultural values are driven by that society's technology, not by humanity itself.

Bostrom argues that transhumanism does not entail technological optimism. He regularly points to the risks of potential harm, including the 'extreme possibility of intelligent life becoming extinct'. Less dramatic negative consequences include even greater social inequalities, the gradual loss of personal human relationships and human agency, and continued loss of environmental health and biodiversity.

There are multiple ideological currents within the techno-transhumanism movement. Not all are in agreement, nor do they share Bostrom's circumspect view. The currents include extreme techno-utopianism at one end of the spectrum (such as paradise-engineering, singularitarianism, and artificial super-intelligence), and more moderate and risk-aware views (such as democratic and theoretical transhumanism) at the other end. The transhumanism movement has also attracted some fringe elements, such as bio-punks, cyber-punks, and bio-hackers. We must wonder how different these 21st-century techno-enhancement theories are, ethically, from Comte and Spencer's 19th-century social engineering.

Posthumanism as superman complex

The term posthumanism is used in a variety of ways in different contexts. For Bostrom a posthuman person is one with at least one posthuman capacity, meaning 'a general central capacity greatly exceeding the maximum attainable by any current human being without recourse to new technological means'. By general central capacity he means healthspan, cognition, and emotion. Because posthumanism requires technological intervention, posthumans are essentially a new, or hybrid, species. Related concepts include cyborg and android. The term cyborg is a shortened form of 'cybernetic organism' and arose out of cybernetics in the 1960s. However, the concept of a human/machine hybrid has been used in science fiction for almost 200 years, originating with Mary Shelley's Frankenstein monster. The android is a robot in the form of a human being (see Figure 12). This concept is connected with the more recent high-tech movement to create so-called machine super-intelligence. The movie character Terminator is a cyborg.

The most vocal of high-tech transhumanists have ambitions that seem to have grown out of the superman trope so dominant in early to mid-20th-century North America. Their version of transhumanism includes the idea that human functioning can be technologically enhanced exponentially, until the eventual convergence of human and machine into the singularity or posthumanism. The singularity refers to an artificial super-intelligence (ASI) greater than human intelligence. Bostrom eschews the use of the word singularity, claiming 'the term singularity…has been used confusedly in many disparate senses and has accreted an unholy (yet almost millenarian) aura of techno-utopian connotations'. He prefers to focus on the prospect of machine super-intelligence, warning of the dangers and discussing strategies for how to deal with it to reduce the potential existential risk.

The idea of something like a future singularity (humans transcending biology) is not new. Science fiction writer and mathematics professor Verner Vinge introduced the idea of singularity at the VISION-21 Symposium sponsored by NASA Lewis Research Center in 1993. He claimed that John von Neumann had already spoken in the 1950s of a coming technological singularity, beyond which human affairs as we know them would finish, as a result of the ever accelerating progress of technology.

Vinge predicted that we would have the technological means to create superhuman intelligence between 2005 and 2030, arguing this would end the human era.

Google engineer Ray Kurzweil has attempted to popularize the singularity concept. Not surprisingly, Kurzweil's predicted date for the appearance of the Singularity, 2029, sits nicely within Vinge's dates. Is it coincidence that the cyborg assassin from the movie Terminator was sent back to restore order in the year 2029? To further promote the concept Kurzweil co-founded the Singularity University in Silicon Valley in 2009 with Peter Diamandis. The espoused mission of Singularity University is to use accelerating technologies to address 'humanity's hardest problems'. A clue to their extreme techno-topianism is that they see humans as a multi-planetary species and aim to colonize other planets (like Mars) offering humans a 'kind of species survival insurance policy against extinction-level events'. Kurzweil refers to the singularity as an inevitable empirical trend but his mission reads like a science fiction screenplay. It is hard to overlook the striking resemblance between the Singularity University logo and the Superman logo.

When unleashing accelerating technologies, we need to ask ourselves, how should we distinguish between authentic projects to aid humanity, and highly resourced messianic hubris? Clarke pre-empted these developments in 1979:

> The tale of the future is the dreamtime of industrial society. It reaches down to the mythic roots within human experience to find sources of supreme power, means of transcending all limitations, opportunities for achieving absolute perfection.

The fifth AI winter

Much of the transhumanist discourse of the 21st century reflects a historical and sociological naivety. Other than Bostrom, transhumanist writers seem oblivious to the 3,000-year history of humanity's attempts to predict, control, and understand the future. Although many transhumanists sit squarely within a cornucopian narrative, they seem unaware of the alternating historical waves of techno-utopianism (or Cornucopianism) and techno-dystopianism (or Malthusianism).

Neo-Cornucopianism is unbridled optimism about the abilities of technology to fix everything. It is called 'the techno-fix solution' in critical futures literature and includes among its ranks Kurzweil, Pearce, and Byron Reese. Kurzweil claims that humans can and will take positive advantage of technology, and that it will not replace us but improve and extend our lives. Pearce describes his paradise engineering in his book *The Hedonistic Imperative*, in which he argues for a biological programme to eliminate all forms of cruelty, suffering, and malaise. Pearce's approach involving genetic engineering and nanotechnology sounds very much like a 21st-century version of social Darwinism. Reese believes the Internet and technology will end 'Ignorance, Disease, Poverty, Hunger and War' and we will colonize outer space with a billion other planets each populated with a billion people. In his science fiction-like book *Infinite Progress* Reese claims:

> We will launch terra-forming nanites into space that land on lifeless rocks and planets and transform them, at the atomic level, to be filled with carbon, hydrogen, oxygen, and everything else we might need. Atmospheres will form, then plants will be seeded, and the colonists will arrive.

Neo-Malthusians are pessimistic about population growth, environment, climate, and the future. Important 20th-century books include Paul Ehrlich's (1968) *The Population Bomb* and *Limits to Growth* (1972) report to the Club of Rome. Bashford claims that Julian Huxley was a Malthusian.

As the exponential growth in the technologies associated with robotics and AI parallels the rise in global acts of terrorism, scientists, philosophers, and AI funders are sending out sharp warnings. Bostrom's book *Superintelligence: Paths, Dangers, Strategies* (2014) is the most comprehensive discussion of the issues so far. Bostrom provides a detailed overview of the history of attempts at artificial intelligence, the modes of possibility for its development, the likelihood of success, and the risks and dangers. Theoretical physicist and mathematician Stephen Hawking has been outspoken on his fears about the dire consequences of future 'superintelligent creations', which could match or surpass humans' current abilities. His concern is that if the development of full artificial intelligence is achieved, it could spell the end of the human race. Elon Musk, Tesla and SpaceX founder, has spoken out about his concerns at MIT Aeronautics and Astronautics Department's Centennial Symposium (2014). Musk, a former enthusiast, warned that artificial intelligence could be our biggest existential threat. He has called for regulatory oversight at national or international level and granted millions to research. Like Bostrom, Hawking, and Musk, some of the early-adopter Neo-Cornucopians are becoming very vocal about the existential risks ahead. Jaron Lanier, known as the 'dean of the digital dissenters', refers to himself as the first guy to sober up after a heavy-duty party. In a scathing critique of the culture of Silicon Valley, Lanier claims it 'treats humans like electrical rays in a vast machine'. With Silicon Valley being the home of many of the new tech-billionaires, and now a US Department of Defense office, this is a sobering thought.

Research on killer apps discussed by Allenby and Sarewitz show there is good reason for concern. The 19th-century tensions between Malthusians and Cornucopians are set to repeat themselves in response to high-tech transhumanism.

In an interesting counter-intuitive development, Bostrom points out that since the 1950s there have been periods of hype and high expectations about the prospect of AI (1950s, 1970s, 1980s, 1990s) each followed by a period of setback and disappointment that he calls an 'AI winter'. The surge of hype and enthusiasm about the coming singularity surrounding Kurzweil's simplistic beliefs about replicating human consciousness may be about to experience a fifth AI winter.

The dehumanization critique

The strongest critiques of the overextension of technology involve claims of dehumanization, and these arguments are not new. Canadian philosopher of the electronic age Marshall McLuhan was primarily a techno-utopian, but he was also a critical thinker, who cautioned decades ago against too much human extension into technology. McLuhan famously claimed that every media extension of man is an amputation. For example, once we have a car, we don't walk to the shops any more; once we have a computer hard-drive we don't have to remember things; and now we have personal GPS on our cell phones no one can find their way about without it. Based on McLuhan's philosophy, we are becoming post-literate because we rely on screens full of pictures, rather than print media, such as books. It is thus possible that extensions of human faculties, through techno- and bio-enhancement, will bring about arrested development in the natural evolution of higher human faculties.

Lewis Mumford's critique of the dangers of too much technological extension was grounded in his organic humanism. As part of this approach Mumford considered that the space exploration of his era was a form of technological exhibitionism. I wonder what he would think of Kurzweil's plans to colonize Mars, and Reese's vision to launch terra-forming nanites into space? But perhaps these nanites will meet a swarm of surveillance cyborg insects on their travels. In his book *Values for Survival* (1946) Mumford made his humanistic priorities clear:

> If we are to create balanced human beings, capable of entering into world-wide co-operation with all other men of good will...we must give as much weight to the arousal of the emotions and to the expression of moral and esthetic values as we now give to science, to invention, to practical organization.

From the perspective of psychology of intelligence the term artificial intelligence is an oxymoron. Intelligence, by nature, cannot be artificial and its inestimable complexity defies any notion of artificiality. We need the courage to name the notion of 'machine intelligence' for what it really is: anthropomorphism. Until AI researchers can define what they mean by intelligence, and explain how it relates to consciousness, the term artificial intelligence must remain a word without universal meaning. At best, so-called artificial intelligence can mean little more than machine capability. As for the newly minted machine *super*-intelligence it is difficult not to read this as unbridled hubris.

Chapter 5
Technotopian or human-centred futures?

Contrasting futures for humanity

A vital question with regard to the future is how we deal with human futures. While high-tech futures are of interest to some futurists, many futures scholars are focused on the potential social, cultural, and environmental impacts of rapid unprecedented change, including exponential technological developments.

We are at a critical point today in research into human futures. Two divergent streams show up in the human futures conversations. Which direction we choose will also decide the fate of earth futures—at least in the sense of earth's dual role as home for humans, and habitat for life in general. As a psychologist and educator, I am well aware that the domain of human futures is extremely complex and that creating binaries is an oversimplification. However, I choose to deliberately oversimplify here to make a point that I believe is vital.

My approach is informed by Oliver Markley and Willis Harman's work *Changing Images of Man* (1982) in which they draw attention to two contrasting future images of human development: 'evolutionary transformational' and 'technological extrapolationist'. I realize that the two types of utopian human futures distinguished by Polak in *The Image of the Future* (1955) provide historical lineages for these streams, as does C. P. Snow's 'Two Cultures' (the humanities and the sciences). Sociologist Menno Boldt explores values and goals that might define a person who wants to create better earthly conditions for humanity. In *A Quest for Humanity* (2011) Boldt prioritizes respect for the dignity of every human being and identifies qualities to be found in what he calls a 'transcendent humanity'. The qualities he includes are empathy, generosity, fairness, and forgiveness, as well as a commitment to working for peace and opposing the use of violence and destruction.

I am interested in how these different values are likely to play out in human futures, especially with respect to long-term consequences. Building on Markley and Harman's images, and Boldt's set of qualities for the transcendent human, I offer two contrasting approaches to human futures and their inherent values and ethics. Any approach to human futures is invariably informed by our image of the human being.

What I call 'human-centred futures' is humanitarian, philosophical, and ecological. It is based on a view of humans as kind, fair, consciously evolving, peaceful agents of change with a responsibility to maintain the ecological balance between humans, earth, and cosmos. Human-centred futures involve ongoing psychological, socio-cultural, aesthetic, and spiritual development, and a commitment to the betterment of earthly conditions for all humanity through education, cultural diversity, greater economic and resource parity, and respect for future generations.

By contrast, what I call 'technotopian futures' is dehumanizing, scientistic, and atomistic. It is based on a mechanistic, behaviourist model of the human being, with a thin cybernetic view of intelligence. The transhumanist ambition to create future techno-humans is anti-human and anti-evolutionary. It involves technological, biological, and genetic enhancement of humans and artificial machine intelligence. Some technotopians have transcendental dreams of abandoning earth to build a fantasized techno-heaven on Mars or in satellite cities in outer space.

This contest for the control of human futures is not new. It has been waged intermittently since at least the European Enlightenment. Because of the extreme existential risks facing humanity, it is necessary to detour backwards to appreciate how this struggle between techno-centred and human-centred futures began.

The Enlightenment contest for human futures

> Our hopes, as to the future condition of the human species, may be reduced to three points: the destruction of inequality between different nations; the progress of equality in one and the same nation, and lastly, the real improvement of man.

This quote by Flechtheim is the more remarkable when we realize that it was said over 220 years ago. Flechtheim is quoting French philosopher the Marquis de Condorcet (1743–94), who, when facing death in 1793–4 in the wake of the French Revolution, wrote *Sketch for a Historical Picture of the Progress of the Human Mind*. A key contributor to the French Enlightenment, and holding similar views to many of the German idealist and romantic philosophers, de Condorcet envisioned humans as progressing towards a perfectly utopian society. Given the exchange of ideas among French and German philosophers at the time, it is highly likely that de Condorcet was influenced by German romantic philosopher Johann Gottfried (von) Herder's *This Too a Philosophy of History for the Formation of Humanity* published just twenty years earlier. In his treatise on the evolution of human consciousness, Herder claimed, 'there exist radical mental differences between historical periods, that people's concepts, beliefs, sensations, etc. differ in important ways from one period to another'. Along with German idealist and romantic philosophers, de Condorcet was a forerunner of humanistic futures thinking.

The German romantic philosopher who stood out as a pioneer of futures thinking in the High Romantic period is Georg Philipp Friedrich von Hardenberg (1772–1801). His pen name was Novalis meaning 'that which is of the future'. One of his many projects, although it remained incomplete at the end of his short life of less than thirty years, was his *Enzyklopädistik*. As noted by Novalis scholar Chad Wellmon: 'Operating at the boundaries of the possible, the ideal, and the real, Novalis's Enzyklopädistik both reflects on the conditions of possibility of an encyclopedia and actually attempts to make one.' Novalis's mode of working 'at the boundaries of the possible, the ideal and the real' was an uncanny forerunner of current notions of possible, preferred, and probable futures. In Wellmon's view, Novalis's encyclopedia was about creating 'an anticipatory project, possible, unfinished and a future to come…an encyclopedic way of knowing'. Novalis was anticipating the emergence of both futures studies and the integral worldview in the 20th to 21st centuries. As part of his theory of cultural evolution, Novalis envisaged three ages in the social development of humanity. The kings and priests led the first. Politicians and economists led the second age, whilst the third (the emergent one) is to be led by interdependent individuals with the gift of 'inspired artistic imagination'. The third age in social development would have the characteristics of liberty, equality, and fraternity, the ideals of the French Revolution, which so inspired Novalis.

Herder, de Condorcet, and Novalis would most likely have read two other important works of their era. The first, *L'Homme machine* (1748) (*Man as Machine*) published by Julien Offray de La Mettrie (1709–51), radically overturned previous views of the human being. Although not considered scientific at the time, the mechanistic view of human nature put forward by La Mettrie cast a long shadow into the future. It influenced B. F. Skinner's 20th-century psychology school of radical behaviourism, the cybernetic view of human consciousness, and contemporary branches of transhumanism. The second was *A Philosophical Review of the Successive Advances of the Human Mind* by French economist Anne Robert Jacques Turgot (1727–81). Published just two years later, Turgot's holistic view of humanity, incorporating various social and cultural dimensions, was in sharp contrast to La Mettrie's mechanistic theory of human nature.

The striking similarity between the titles of the works by de Condorcet and Turgot cannot be mere coincidence. These French and German philosophers (Turgot, de Condorcet, Herder, and Novalis) shared a belief in human development as a humanistic ideal, interwoven with culture, society, education, and the arts. They diverged, however, in ways that reflected an important differentiation between the French and German Enlightenment. This is relevant to the two streams we see today.

Over that fifty-year time span in the second half of the 18th century, we can see the beginnings of the power struggle for human futures, between human-centred values and the dehumanization that was taking hold with the Industrial Revolution.

The German philosophical stream included the idealists and romantics, such as Herder, Novalis, Goethe, Hegel, and Schelling. They took their lineage from Leibniz and his 17th-century integral, spiritually based evolutionary work. These German philosophers seeded a spiritual-evolutionary humanism that laid down important foundations for the human-centred futures approach presented here.

The French philosophical influence included La Mettrie's mechanistic man and René Descartes's early 17th-century split between mind and body, forming the basis of French (or Cartesian) Rationalism. These French philosophers (La Mettrie, Descartes, Turgot, and de Condorcet) were secular humanists. Secular humanism is one lineage of technotopian futures. Scientific positivism is another.

Origins of a humanistic transhumanism

In 1950, Pierre Teilhard de Chardin (1881–1955) published the essay *From the Pre-Human to the Ultra-Human: The Phases of a Living Planet*, in which he speaks of 'some sort of Trans-Human at the ultimate heart of things'. Teilhard de Chardin's Ultra-Human and Trans-Human were evolutionary concepts linked with spiritual/human futures. These concepts inspired his friend Julian Huxley to write about transhumanism, which he did in 1957 as follows (Huxley's italics):

> The human species can, if it wishes, transcend itself—not just sporadically, an individual here in one way, an individual there in another way—but in its entirety, as humanity. We need a name for this new belief. Perhaps *transhumanism* will serve: man remaining man, but transcending himself, by realizing new possibilities of and for his human nature.

This quote of Julian Huxley, while frequently used to attribute to him the coining of the term transhumanism, has sparked some controversy. Some contemporary transhumanists have incorrectly cited the quote as being associated with a 1927 Huxley publication, others have ignored Huxley's contribution to the discourse altogether. Peter Harrison and Joseph Wolniak claim in their *History of Transhumanism* (2015) that the term was actually coined in 1940 by a Canadian historian, W. D. Lighthall, who draws from Dante's *Divine Comedy* and biblical references to make a case for the apostle 'Paul's Transhumanism'.

Regardless of who first coined the term, the high-tech transhumanism that developed in the late 20th century has taken off in another direction entirely. It bears little resemblance to Huxley's transhumanism, which is deeply imbued with humanistic values. Nor does it relate to Lighthall's transhumanism, which seems to be more closely linked with religious concepts such as the Christian glorification of the body. Putting these ideas aside I want to explore the contrast between Huxley's human-centred transhumanism and contemporary, technotopian transhumanism.

Huxley, a biologist and humanitarian, was the first Director-General of UNESCO in 1946, and the first President of the British Humanist Association. Huxley's transhumanism was more humanistic and spiritual than technological, inspired by Teilhard de Chardin's spiritually evolved human. Notably, Huxley wrote the introduction to Teilhard de Chardin's *The Phenomenon of Man* (1959).

Cambridge historian Alison Bashford points to two ways in which Huxley's transhumanism differed from contemporary transhumanism. First, Huxley was committed to the evolutionary imperative for all humans, not just particular individuals or populations, and secondly, his transhumanism was based on social not technological improvements through increased opportunities for all in education and health services. She notes: 'His humanism and even his transhumanism once he started using that term, was always based on what he called evolutionary humanism.' Huxley put forward notions of planetary evolution, along the lines of Teilhard de Chardin's notion of the planetization of mankind. He also promoted the idea of conscious evolution, which originated with the German romantic philosopher Schelling, but did not become a popular idea until the late 20th century.

An interesting wild card possibility is that humanists will reclaim the concept of the transhuman to reflect its origins in the evolutionary humanism of Teilhard de Chardin and Huxley. Echoing Menno Boldt's 'transcendent humanity', French social theorist and presidential adviser Jacques Attali attempts to reclaim transhumanism in such a way in his book *A Brief History of the Future*:

Transhumans will be altruistic, a citizen of the planet, at once nomadic and sedentary, his neighbor's equal in rights and obligations, hospitable and respectful of the world. Together, transhumans will give birth to planetary institutions and change the course of industrial enterprises.

Evolving superhuman beings

The evolutionary ideas that were in discussion the century before Darwin were focused on consciousness and theories of human progress as a cultural, aesthetic, and spiritual ideal. These late 18th-century German philosophers foreshadowed the 20th-century human potential and positive psychology movements. To support their evolutionary ideals for society they created a universal education system, the aim of which was to develop the whole person (*Bildung* in German).

After Darwin, philosophers began to explore the impact of Darwinian evolution on human futures, in other ways than Spencer's social Darwinism. Friedrich Nietzsche wrote about the *Übermensch*, in *Thus Spoke Zarathustra* (1883). His concept has been translated from the German with several meanings: 'Overman, Overhuman, Above-Human, Superman, Super-human, Ultrahuman, Higher-Person, Higher-Being.' His ideas about the higher person were informed by Darwin's biological evolution and the idealist writings on evolution of consciousness. His Übermensch was also deeply connected to his ideas on freedom.

French philosopher Henri Bergson's contribution to the superhuman discourse first appeared in *Creative Evolution* (1907). Although Bergson did not directly cite Nietzsche's work, his work had its roots in Nietzsche's Übermensch. Like Nietzsche, Bergson saw the superman arising out of the human being, in much the same way that humans have arisen from animals. Rudolf Steiner, in his own research on evolution of consciousness, discussed the superman theories of both Nietzsche and Bergson. Nietzsche's notion of the superman was paraphrased by Steiner as 'The animal bore man in itself; must not man bear within himself a higher being, the *superman*?'

In parallel with the efforts of Nietzsche and Bergson, Steiner articulated his own ideas on evolving human-centred futures, with concepts such as spirit self and spirit man (between 1904 and 1925). During the same period, Aurobindo Ghose, an Indian political activist, was writing in India about the Overman as a type of consciously evolving future human being. Sri Aurobindo's integral evolutionary work drew from both the ancient Hindu texts and German idealist philosophy. Both Steiner and Aurobindo founded education systems after the *Bildung* style of holistic human development.

Analogous with the two streams of transhumanism—the techno- and the spiritual-humanistic—Teilhard de Chardin wrote about a spiritual forerunner, and humanistic counterpoint, to the technological concept of the singularity. Teilhard de Chardin's Omega Point reflects a belief that the universe is evolving toward a higher level of material complexity and spiritual consciousness. The Omega Point–Singularity tension is a touchstone for further research into human futures.

Reinventing human-centred time

The 2,500-year-old concept of linear time has itself undergone evolutionary change since Ancient Greece. What began as the more formal measurement of already recognized cosmological and natural cycles became gradually stripped of its natural and cosmological dimension. After the Industrial Revolution linear time further contracted into factory time. As time became entrapped in the industrial machine, humans came under the spell of mechanical notions of time.

However, this predictable, mechanical, conception of time began to unravel with the elaboration of Einstein's theory of special relativity and the discovery of quantum mechanics in the early 1900s. Time was no longer an object, upon which the movement or change of things can be measured in discrete, identical fragments. The new scientific discoveries had huge philosophical implications, gradually displacing fixed concepts of linear time with radically new concepts.

German phenomenologist Edmund Husserl developed the idea of 'subjective time'—the time of the soul—in contrast to external or objective time. Following Husserl's phenomenological explorations of time, Martin Heidegger spoke of the notion of 'existential time'. British philosopher Whitehead applied his process view of thinking to time and Bergson described the paradoxical notion of time as *durée* (the conscious flow of life). Bergson's views of time as having a radical multiplicity sit well with the notion of multiple futures. Husserl, with his concept of subjective time, was the first to take into account the personal, or psychological, aspect of time. Even within futures studies this psychological aspect is under-developed and needs to be further researched. Like quantum mechanics and chaos theory, these new concepts will take time to trickle into mainstream thinking.

Other societal developments have contributed to our changing sense of time throughout the last century. Accelerating technology has extended the old divisions of seconds, minutes, and hours into nanoseconds at one extreme and radioactive half-life at the other. Industrial era time is dominated by politics and economics and these metaphors dominate everyday conversations, with such phrases as 'time is money', or 'buying time'. The speed addiction of the present age can be seen in fast food outlets, instant communications, and the culture of over-consumption. The speeding up of time means that the future now rushes towards us in a hurry!

Yet life today is not simple and one-dimensional. In contrast to the accelerating anxiety and time panic of the 21st century, counter-trends are emerging, such as the slow movement and the retro travel movement. The old concept of cyclical time is being reclaimed from both non-Western and feminist perspectives. These emerging issues suggest a gradual move to re-examine our relationship with time and rediscover time's multifaceted relationship with nature and cosmos that has been hidden in plain sight while time was tied to the industrial era worldview.

Conscious human-centred futures

From a human-centred perspective on consciously evolving human futures there have been several important 20th-century developments. Increasingly in the last fifty years, evolutionary change can be found in most of the major academic disciplines. I have coined the term 'megatrends of the mind' for these developments. They are indications of the evolution of consciousness, which Ervin László claims 'has become a pre-condition of our collective survival'.

An environmental scan of the major fields of knowledge shows new ways of thinking have emerged within science, philosophy, psychology, and education. In science we can observe the early 20th-century scientific turn from classical physics to quantum physics, followed by the shift from the closed system of classical physics to the open systems of postclassical biology, chaos, and complexity sciences. A similar transition can be found in Western philosophical thought from modernism to postmodernism and poststructuralism. The singular notion of philosophy, implying British analytic philosophy, has expanded into a philosophical pluralism that acknowledges comparative, process, and integral philosophies. Over the last fifty years psychology has extended beyond the clinical, empiricist, and behaviourist models to new approaches that include humanistic, transpersonal, developmental, and postformal psychology theories. Evolutionary waves of change can even be observed in the stalwart discipline of education. The factory model of formal schooling designed for the 19th century is being challenged by innovative, postformal pedagogies better suited to the 21st century.

The movement to counterbalance the excesses of fragmentation associated with disciplinary specialization is well established via inter-, multi-, and transdisciplinary approaches. It is part of more integrated futures of knowledge creation.

Three major bodies of research offer counterpoints to the techno-transhumanist claim that superhuman powers can only be reached through technological, biological, or genetic enhancement. They show that humans may have far greater capacities across several domains than we realize. In brief these themes are the future of the body, cultural futures, and futures of thinking.

Contemporary research points to the superhuman potential already available within us. Michael Murphy's book *The Future of the Body* documents 'superhuman powers' unrelated to technological or biological enhancement. For forty years Murphy, founder of Esalen Institute, has been researching what he calls a *Natural History of Supernormal Attributes*. He has developed an archive of 10,000 studies of individual humans, throughout history, who have demonstrated supernormal experiences. Expanding considerably on Bostrom's three categories of 'healthspan...cognition...emotion', Murphy's classification includes twelve groups of attributes:

> Perceptual abilities, kinesthetic awareness and self-regulation, communication abilities, vitality, movement abilities, abilities to alter the environment, capacities for pain and pleasure, cognition, volition, sense of self, love, and bodily structures and processes.

In almost 800 pages Murphy documents the supernormal capacities of humans as diverse as Catholic mystics, Sufi ecstatics, Hindi-Buddhist siddhis, martial arts practitioners, and elite athletes. Murphy concludes that these extreme examples are the 'developing limbs and organs of our evolving human nature'. We also know from the examples of savants, extreme sport and adventure, and narratives of mystics and saints from a variety of religions, that we humans are always extending ourselves.

Is it possible that the obsession with techno-enhancement is preventing us from consciously evolving our inherent super-human potential? It is certainly the case that many young people are showing signs of addiction to their mobile phones and computers. Evidence of this includes the appearance of digital detox clinics and the emerging issue of Internet addiction disorder.

Regarding cultural evolution, throughout the 20th century, numerous scholars and writers have put forward ideas about human futures drawing on the German idealists, Teilhard de Chardin, Gebser, and others. Contemporaries include Ervin László, who links evolution of consciousness with global planetary shifts; Duane Elgin, who writes about the evolution and futures of society; Richard Tarnas, whose book *The Passions of the Western Mind* traces socio-cultural developments over the last 2,000 years, pointing to emergent changes; and Habermas, whose book *Communication and the Evolution of Society* suggests a similar developmental pattern. In the late 1990s Duane Elgin and Coleen LeDrew undertook a forty-three-nation World Values Survey, including Scandinavia, Switzerland, Britain, Canada, and the United States. They concluded, 'a new global culture and consciousness have taken root and are beginning to grow in the world'. They called it the postmodern shift and described it as having two qualities. The first was the ecological perspective which they saw as a 'spacious perspective, [through which] the

Earth (and even the cosmos) are seen as interconnected, living systems'. The second was a self-reflexive ability to step back from the rush of life. These qualities may be behind the slow-time, retro travel, and other emerging movements, and lead us directly into postformal reasoning.

Adult developmental psychology research builds on positive psychology, and the human potential movement beginning with Abraham Maslow's book *Further Reaches of Human Nature* (1971). In combination with transpersonal psychology the research is rich with extended views of human futures in cognitive, emotional, and spiritual domains. For four decades adult developmental psychology researchers such as Michael Commons, Jan Sinnott, and Lawrence Kohlberg have been researching the systematic, pluralistic, complex, and integrated thinking of mature adults. They call this mature thought 'postformal reasoning' and their research provides valuable insights into higher modes of reasoning that are central to the discourse on futures of thinking. Some of the features that these psychologists identify include complex paradoxical thinking, creativity and imagination, relativism and pluralism, self-reflection and ability to dialogue, and intuition. Wilber's integral psychology research is integrated with his cultural history research to build a significantly enhanced image of the potential for consciously evolving human futures. I have applied these findings to education in *Postformal Education: A Philosophy for Complex Futures*.

Given the breadth and subtlety of postformal reasoning that is available for us to develop, how likely is it that machines could ever acquire such higher functioning human features as these? The technotopians discussing artificial superhuman intelligence carefully avoid the consciousness question. Bostrom explains that all the machine intelligence systems currently in use operate in a very *narrow* range of human cognitive capacity (weak AI). Even at its most ambitious, it is limited to trying to replicate 'abstract reasoning and general problem-solving skills' (strong AI). ASI proponents seem unaware of the research on evolution of consciousness, metaphysics of mind, or philosophies and psychologies of consciousness showing that human intelligence is continually evolving.

Even if techno-developers succeed in replicating general intelligence, at best it would function as Jean Piaget's formal operations albeit with greater processing speed. We now know from the adult developmental psychologists that mature, high-functioning adults are capable of complex, postformal reasoning. It is questionable whether anyone working with AI is aware of the limits of formal reasoning let alone that there are higher stages of postformal reasoning. And what do they know of Howard Gardner's theories of multiple (human) intelligences? There is no evidence in the literature on AI that the theories about higher-level reasoning are being addressed.

These developments in thinking and systems of knowledge represent a major shift from the industrial worldview associated with positivism, modernism, and Piaget's formal reasoning, to the post-industrial worldviews of post-positivism, postmodernism, and postformal reasoning. If we look towards the longer-term futures of thinking we can expect to see more of the features of postformal reasoning appearing. Although this evolutionary aspect is rarely explicitly included in the futures literature, futures scholars and researchers are not immune to these influences. The mind-set shift is slowly trickling into the futures discourse. Hideg points to a new evolutionary paradigm of futures studies emerging at the end of the 20th century.

When all of this research is taken together it indicates that we humans are already becoming capable of far greater powers of mind, emotion, body, and spirit than previously imagined. If we seriously want to develop superhuman intelligence and powers in the 21st century and beyond we have two options. We can continue to invest heavily in our technotopian dreams of creating machines that can operate better than humans. Or we can invest more of our consciousness and resources on educating and consciously evolving human futures with all the wisdom that would entail.

The human futures terrain is vast and complex, and this chapter should be read as the beginning of a conversation that has barely begun.

Chapter 6
Grand global futures challenges

Canvassing global perspectives

Anyone who thinks deeply and looks beyond their own household will see a large number of global challenges as unpredictable futures rush towards us. The challenges we face for near and long-term futures have been called a crisis of crises. They range across the gamut of socio-cultural, geo-political, and environmental domains. Bearing in mind that all these challenges are complex and systemically interconnected, this chapter offers multiple starting points for further dialogue. Futurists discuss the grand global challenges from a variety of perspectives.

James Dator calls them the 'Unholy Trinity, Plus One'. Dator's Unholy Trinity is the end of cheap and abundant oil; multiple environmental challenges; and global economic and fiscal collapse. Dator's Plus One is lack of adequate government intervention. Jorgen Randers claims that a sustainability revolution is under way, but that it will take most of this century to complete. He identifies five big issues, which are inextricably linked with the sustainability revolution and its likelihood of success. His big issues are the end of capitalism, the end of economic growth, the end of slow democracy, the end of generational harmony, and the end of stable climate. Futurist, ethical economics expert, and author Hazel Henderson also focuses on one central transition. In her 2014 monograph *Mapping the Global Transition to the Solar Age*, Henderson highlights the transition from the obsolete industrial era mind-set to an emerging solar age as a path to a 'more green and sustainable economic future'.

In *All Tomorrow's Crises* Kreibich identifies ten critical megatrends (including pressures on the environment through indiscriminate exploitation of natural resources, population growth and demographic change, globalization of industry, and increased global mobility). He also notes ten core global change problems (including climate change, pollution of oceans and atmosphere, threats to food and water security, global epidemics, and increase in non-sustainable lifestyles). Kreibich's concern, that we are ignoring the resources at our disposal, echoes Dator.

> The core problems of global change are even now deeply affecting all areas of life, and although we already have a great deal of knowledge about the future, very little is being done. There is a huge gap between the challenges—even crises—that we know lie ahead and the practical responses offered on the global, national, and regional levels.

Glenn and Gordon from the Millennium Project (MP) use '15 Global Challenges' as a useful framework to assess global and local prospects for humanity. They include environmental issues such as sustainable development and climate change, clean water and energy; social issues such as population and resources, rich–poor gap, education and learning, status of women and health; science and technology including global convergence of IT; and geo-political issues such as global ethics, transnational organized crime, peace and conflict, democratization, and global foresight and decision-making. Their continuous research with over 4,000 global experts has been reported annually since 1996 in the MP *State of the Future Report*.

The World Economic Forum publishes an *Outlook on the Global Agenda Report* each year with ten trends that will have the biggest impact on the world short-term (twelve to eighteen months). Introducing the 2015 report Al Gore noted the inextricable links between the two dominant issues, economic and environmental. In summary:

> Today, we see the consequences of short-term economic thinking and the reckless use of our planet's resources: water disputes between neighbouring nations, more frequent and powerful extreme weather events brought on by our warming climate, an on-going global deforestation crisis, a rapidly acidifying ocean, eroding topsoil and agricultural capacity, and an alarming biodiversity crisis unparalleled in modern history.

Based on these global perspectives, and my own research and analysis, I synthesize the major global futures challenges into twelve clusters of issues across three broad domains: environmental, geo-political, and socio-cultural. My first mind-map (see Figure 13) includes current trends likely to create major problems for futures of humanity. In a second mind-map I include counter-trends, twists, and surprises (see Figure 14). These alternative futures have potential to mitigate, disrupt, or even reverse the dominant trends and enable others to imagine and create alternatives to the disturbing trends being forecast. Then I focus on Three Grand Global Challenges: growing urbanization, lack of (or inadequate) education, and climate crisis.

Environmental trends and surprises

In the broad environmental domain ecosystem, energy systems and climate crisis are clearly interconnected. I include health because healthy human futures are so reliant on how we deal with the future of our earth, its atmosphere, biosphere, climate, plants, oceans, and sentient beings.

The entire ecosystem of the earth is under severe strain and we have known this for decades. There are widespread concerns

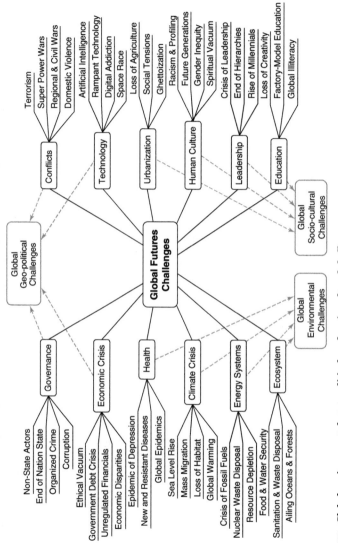

13. **Global environmental, geo-political, and socio-cultural challenges.**

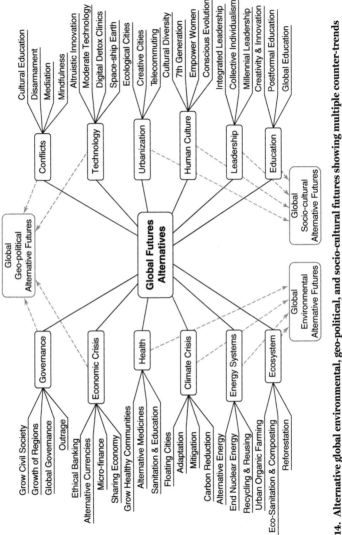

14. **Alternative global environmental, geo-political, and socio-cultural futures showing multiple counter-trends and alternatives to overcome the challenges.**

about food and water security for an expected global population of 9 billion by 2040, based on UN Department of Economic and Social Affairs (DESA) projections 2015–50. Increasing water stress is one of the top ten trends in the World Economic Forum Report for 2015. From an economic and resources perspective, growing urbanization means that rural land is shrinking. Given that rural regions have traditionally supplied most of the food for urban areas, reduced rural land and populations could lead to serious food shortages.

There are many weak signals globally that citizens want to take back control over their food and water security. Attempts to control global food supply by multinationals such as Monsanto are increasingly being resisted by national governments in response to popular demand. Similarly, the Bolivian people successfully took back their urban water supply from corporates in 2000 in a series of protests called the Cochabamba Water War. Cities seeking to creative sustainable solutions are experimenting successfully with vertical gardens, bush food forests, and urban farms, which are part of the growing creative and eco-city movement designed to deal with food security. Cuba embraced and adopted sustainable solutions in its search for political and economic independence after the US embargo. Havana is now a world leader in urban agriculture with more than 50 per cent of its fresh produce grown within the city limits, using organic compost and simple irrigation systems. Organic agriculture, urban gardening, permaculture, herbal medicines, renewable energy, and waste minimization have all developed rapidly since 1990. Signals of a shift from extractive to ecological alternatives to ailing oceans, deforestation, and waste disposal—through reuse and recycling—are weak but not insignificant.

Disturbing energy trends include peak oil and the crisis of fossil fuels, nuclear waste disposal, and overall resource depletion. Welcome counter-trends include the upsurge in renewable energy, the growing awareness of the global need to reuse and recycle, particularly among young people, and the movement to end nuclear energy, because of the near impossibility of eliminating the dangers of waste disposal.

In the global health domain, new and resistant diseases are emerging, some of them threatening to reach pandemic proportions. A global epidemic of mental health problems includes depression, anxiety, and suicide, particularly among the young. In the USA suicide is the third leading cause of death among children aged 10–14 and the second among young people aged 15–34 years. The World Bank claims that depression is a major contributor to the overall global burden of disease. In April 2016 the World Health Organization cited depression as the leading cause of disability, affecting an estimated 350 million people of all ages globally. Counterpoints to these alarming trends include a renewed focus on healthy communities, futures visioning work with young people, alternative and traditional medicines to complement antibiotics, better sanitation in countries most in need, and, last but not least, global educational transformation.

Trends and twists in global power

As part of global power I include the geo-political issues of governance and conflicts, economic issues, and technology—the latter because digital technologies are so ubiquitous that we cannot isolate the power structures from the technologies they are embedded in. Future global governance challenges stem from the shift from a bi-polar (Cold War) world to a multi-polar world (G-20); the rise of non-state actors such as terrorist networks, aided and abetted by the digital revolution; and organized crime and corruption across many levels of global society. There is a paradox with respect to the nation-state: on the one hand there is an intensification of nationalism, which the World Economic Forum (WEF) *Outlook on the Global Agenda Report for 2015* views as a demand for protection against the perceived economic disruption and social dislocation caused by globalization. On the other hand an erosion of power of the nation-state to deal with the complexity of issues leads to a parallel rise in power of city mayors. The tension is evident in the chaos of the British referendum to exit the European Union. The twists and counter-turns in the play of power include growth in high-level global non-government organizations such as the United Nations and its subsidiaries since the end of the Second World War; the emergence of regional geo-political and economic partnerships, such as BRICS (Brazil, Russia, India, China, and South Africa); and the explosion of civil society activism both on the ground and digitally. The Outrage movement is a powerful example of the energy that can be mustered to counter the corruption and abuse of power experienced by everyday citizens.

Economic crisis dominates discussion on global futures challenges. While the media focuses on rising and falling share prices, interest rates, property values, and whether there will be another GFC, another looming economic crisis is largely invisible. In the last few decades the disparity between rich and poor has increased exponentially, both within nations and across the globe. In the WEF *Outlook 2015* 'deepening income inequality' was at number one. In the USA the richest 1 per cent of Americans own 45 per cent of America's wealth, while the bottom 50 per cent of Americans do not own anything. The WEF report indicates that this is not just a problem for developed countries but rather in most countries 'the poorest half of the population often controls less than 10% of its wealth'. While the free market argument is that wealth will trickle down to the needy, in most cases the increasing wealth continues to 'trickle up' to the already wealthy. The WEF research cites improved education as one of the best solutions. On the alternative futures horizon we find the rise of the sharing economy, micro-finance, alternative currencies, the love economy, and ethical banking. None of these will overcome the ethical/moral vacuum lying under the greed of the grasping billionaire minority who must daily turn a blind eye to the needs of the common good. Only individual moral awakening can achieve this.

The shape of conflicts is changing to reflect the geo-political tensions between globalism and nationalism, the growing economic disparity, the rise of non-state actors, and the freedoms and shadows of the digital revolution. As an example, terrorist group ISIS jumped in opportunistically to take advantage of the chaos of the British exit from the European Union. Lone wolf terrorists, who may be isolated psychopaths, claim allegiance to Islamist jihad as a way to justify their crimes. Growing economic disparity is a sleeping giant in terms of potential conflict if disenfranchised populations decide to take united action. Such revolutionary energy of the disenfranchised was amplified digitally in the initial surge of the Arab Spring to overthrow despotic governments. It was largely orchestrated by the millennial generation in North Africa, using Twitter and Facebook. Notwithstanding that, the surge was too weak to sustain itself. Like most violence and conflict, cyber-terrorism has both a geo-political and domestic face. We are only seeing the tip of the iceberg in terms of the socio-cultural and economic impact of emerging issues such as cyber-bullying, cyber-stalking, and identity theft in the domestic arena.

Socio-cultural trends and counter-trends

After brief pointers on the broad domain of human culture and leadership, I focus in more detail on growing urbanization and the failure of education, globally.

Some of the entrenched global challenges in human culture are racism, as found in ethnic and racial profiling; gender inequity; neglect of the rights of future generations; and tensions arising between the extremes of religious fundamentalism and the spiritual vacuum of secularism. A promising cultural counter-trend is the emerging movement to replace GDP growth with growth in well-being as a societal goal.

A vital socio-cultural futures issue is how we care for future generations, the children of our children's children. What kind of earth, environment, tangible and intangible resources are we bequeathing to them? This includes food and water security, safety from war, violence, and toxic environments, and, of course, quality education. Taking a cultural futures lens to future generations, we find the 7th Generation Principle of indigenous peoples, especially of North America. This principle means that elders are guided in their decisions and actions by considering the needs of their descendants, seven generations into the future. This is a wise, futures-oriented principle that has clear benefits for human and earth futures.

The WEF *Outlook 2015* ranked 'lack of leadership' in the top three challenges facing humanity. This crisis of leadership stems from the shift from old hierarchical, militaristic leadership models to new generation collaborative, digital, networked approaches; the rise of millennial post-industrial values; and the sheer complexity of life. Alternatives such as transformational, millennial, and postformal integrated leadership are arising, but will leave a leadership vacuum for some time.

The grand urbanization challenge

Urbanization, the movement of people from rural areas into towns, cities, and, more recently, mega-cities, has been a growing global trend since the beginning of the 20th century. In 1900 only 10 per cent of the global population lived in cities. By 1950 29 per cent of the world's two and half billion people lived in cities. In 2010 the global urban population tipped beyond 50 per cent. In 2014, 54 per cent of the world's population of over seven billion was urbanized. The UN DESA Population Division (2014) projects that by 2050 the 1950 proportions will be reversed with 66 per cent of the global population being urbanized. The picture of growing urbanization is complex, diverse, and heterogeneous and there are emerging counter-trends. First, I want to make a distinction between 'old urbanization' and 'new urbanization' (sometimes called 'new urbanism').

Key drivers of old urbanization over the past fifty years were industrialization and globalization, both motivated by the desire for economic growth. The drivers of the new urbanization include sustainability and the creativity required to build a sustainable post-industrial urbanism that values people and planet over profit. In the coming decades nations of Africa, Asia, and Latin America will continue to play catch-up with the global north. Many do not want to merely copy what the old urban zones were doing fifty years ago, but to keep abreast of the new urbanization drivers: sustainability and creativity.

While sustainability is a goal of the new urbanism it is threatened by growth that is too rapid with insufficient time for basic infrastructures to be developed (such as power and water supplies, sanitation, health services, education, and transportation).

When rapid urbanization occurs in pre-industrial societies, as it has in China, Africa, parts of Latin America, and elsewhere, instead of improved living conditions the UN DESA in its *World Urbanization Prospects: The 2014 Revision* reports the following:

> Hundreds of millions of the world's urban poor live in sub-standard conditions ... [including] rapid sprawl, pollution, and environmental degradation, together with unsustainable production and consumption patterns.

Such rapid growth undermines the three pillars of sustainable development recommended by the Rio+20 United Nations Conference on Sustainable Development in 2012. These are 'economic development, social development and environmental protection'. Rapid urbanization does not generally benefit the whole community equally. Most industrializing nations follow the free-market American model, which brings greater social disparity and poor working and living conditions for disenfranchised immigrant workers, the youth, the elders, and women.

Rapid urbanization also depletes and diminishes the zones of natural vegetation and wilderness that once surrounded cities and provided habitat for diverse species. New forms of regeneration of forests, grasslands, and wetlands need to be developed if we are not to turn the whole earth into a desert. The greening of established cities, like Berlin, Manchester, and New York, can be models for planners in Nigeria and western China so they do not repeat the old mistakes. There is an urgent need for more experienced urban environments to develop sustainable cities policies so that newly urbanizing regions can benefit from the hard experience of the old industrialized nations. In a globalized, interconnected world, there is no excuse for ignorance. Cities can form alliances and networks for knowledge sharing about paths to sustainability and resource management. Internet technology can be used to disseminate research and knowledge about more socially and politically equitable forms of urbanization, as we find in Scandinavian countries. However, lack of access to technology can be a consequence for those remaining in rural regions.

Efforts towards sustainable urban development in emerging nations show mixed success. Masdar City, Abu Dhabi, UAE, is due for completion in 2025 and aims to be one of the world's most sustainable, low-carbon, low-waste cities. China and Singapore are collaborating on an eco-city project, Tianjin City, designed to be a model of sustainable urban development throughout Asia and the world, planned for completion in 2020. While the reality of these cities is falling short of the ideal it is welcome to see sustainability principles being attempted globally.

The creative city movement is a counter-trend that will shape the way cities urbanize in coming decades, supported by the Creative Cities Network, a UNESCO partner. In *Creative City* (2007) Maurizio Carta points to three design dimensions: 'culture, communication and cooperation, which support the development of a creative class, and contribute to urban regeneration and sustainability'. These validate Richard Florida's 'creative class' and Paul Ray's 'cultural creatives'.

Some Latin American nations are examples of wise urbanization using sustainable and creative approaches to transportation (Curitiba, Brazil) and integrated social practices introduced by Mayor Enrique Peñalosa between 1998 and 2001 (Bogotá, Colombia). In Australia the desire to own a large suburban house and land is wilting before the cultural attraction of post-industrial chic, inner-urban regeneration of factories and warehouses. Creativity is central to transforming cities from black and dirty industrial wastelands to green and sustainable creative cultural hubs such as Berlin and Manchester. The post-industrial counter-trend is welcomed by millennials with their creative, green, and collaborative values. In this context, post-industrial refers to value clusters connected with creative, sustainable, and wise urbanization, rather than an outright rejection of industrialization.

The grand education challenge

Over seventy years ago, the UN Universal Declaration of Human Rights asserted that: 'everyone has a right to education'. In 1990, the World Bank, UNICEF, UNDP, and UNESCO held a World Conference on Education for All in Thailand, creating the 1990 Jomtien World Declaration on Education for All. The Education for All (EFA) project, now run by UNESCO, has had some success in increasing access to schooling for many children and improving literacy rates overall.

However, major challenges remain for the Education for All Agenda. First, there are serious cultural implications of importing one system of education (largely Euro-American) into other cultures. Secondly, it is difficult to assess whether the increased attendance at school is actually increasing learning and life opportunities. Thirdly, it is doubtful that the imported education model will meet the needs of diverse cultural futures in a rapidly changing world.

Between 1990 and 2010 there has been improvement in some areas. In 1990, more than 100 million children had no access to primary schooling. In 2010, there were still almost 61 million primary school-age children out of school, 47 per cent of whom were believed to be unlikely to ever enter school. Over 30 million of the out-of-school children in 2010 lived in sub-Saharan Africa with over half of these being in the category of 'unlikely to ever enter school'. By 2012 another 3 million in the 6- to 11-year age group had entered school. But this is a long way from the UN Millennium Development Goal that 'by 2015, children everywhere, boys and girls alike, will be able to complete a full course of primary schooling'.

The UN declaration of education as a human right was the foremost driver of educational change in recent decades. New drivers have arisen in the higher education sector, which is inextricably caught up in the market forces of globalization and corporatization. Other drivers include the increasing commodification of education associated with the knowledge industry; the information revolution including Massive Open Online Courses (MOOCS); and the rise of the global south.

Educational developments in much of south and western Asia, Latin America, central eastern Europe, and the Arab states are significant. They demonstrate that global education has gathered its own momentum and is no longer just imposed or implanted from the global north. Educational innovation in the global south is self-generating and continues to lower numbers of international students enrolling in Australia, Canada, and the USA.

Looking to the future it is clear that UNESCO with its long-term commitment to human rights is motivated to continue with the Education for All Agenda and will prioritize the most challenged regions, such as sub-Saharan Africa. UNESCO, like other UN agencies and partners, must now shift emphasis from the Millennium Development Goal (MDG) (2000–15) of educational access for all, to the Sustainable Development Goal (SDG) (2015–30) that prioritizes quality education. John Coonrod of The Hunger Project summarized the differences between the two sets of goals as follows:

> The MDGs focused on quantity (eg, high enrollment rates) only to see the quality of education decline in many societies. The SDGs represent the first attempt by the world community to focus on the quality of education—of learning—and the role of education in achieving a more humane world: 'education for sustainable development and sustainable lifestyles, human rights, gender equality, promotion of a culture of peace and non-violence, global citizenship, and appreciation of cultural diversity and of culture's contribution to sustainable development.'

The Education for All project may in the long run overcome the challenge of global illiteracy, but was never designed to deal with the subtle cultural challenge of imposing the Anglo-European industrial era education model on other cultures. Nor are there any easy fixes in sight for emerging educational challenges, particularly in the USA, such as declining creativity among school-aged children and the rise in home-schooling. Home-schooling is being reported as the fastest-growing form of education in the USA with estimates of between two and three million school-aged children being educated at home. While not in itself a problem, when we consider that home-schooling is increasing so dramatically as a result of discontent with mainstream education, it does present a challenge for US educational policy-makers.

The biggest educational futures challenge is not just access. It is how to transform education so it is culturally appropriate and designed to develop whole human beings who are futures-focused and can think creatively about how to deal with emerging challenges. The old fragmented, mechanistic, and materialistic ways of thinking are not capable of dealing with the growing complexity of global environmental, economic, and societal change. Much that is called new knowledge is *not-so-new* knowledge repackaged in new technologies. Creativity, imagination, critical thinking, and complexity are important higher-order cognitive capacities. They are needed to enable the radical rethinking of education that the 21st century demands, if it is to adequately prepare young people for exponential change and uncertainty.

The megatrends of the mind are vitally important for educational futures. Education, along with thinking, needs a complete overhaul, as Edgar Morin argues:

> One of the greatest problems we face today is how to adjust our way of thinking to meet the challenge of an increasingly complex, rapidly changing, unpredictable world. We must rethink our way of organising knowledge.

Not only futurists, but also leading thinkers in many fields (complexity science, ecology, education, integral studies, philosophy, psychology, spirituality studies, and systems theory) attempt to grapple with these challenges. Like Morin, I believe that more complex, self-reflective, organic ways of thinking will be vital in reshaping education, so young people are better equipped for the complexity, paradox, and unpredictability. We urgently need new forms of education based on new thinking, as I write in *Postformal Education: A Philosophy for Complex Futures*:

> While so much has changed out of all recognition in the last hundred years, the institution of formal schooling still resembles the factory schools built to provide human fodder during the Industrial Revolution. Fundamentally, we are still educating our children as if we were living in the 19th century, albeit with a few added digital gadgets, and online infotainment.

The global-societal challenges we face as a species have a huge impact on young people and future generations. The failure of formal schooling to prepare young people to meet those challenges is the subject of much of the critical education literature and more recently fills the pages of education blogs, globally. Global education researchers, practitioners, and policy-makers must tackle the complex global-societal challenges discussed here if education is to contribute to local communities, national priorities, and the global common good.

If we de-link education from economics it can reclaim its place in the socio-cultural domain. Teachers will no longer be primarily child-minders, researchers will not be primarily fund-raisers, and curricula will become focused on the whole-person development of children and young people. Once the profit motive has been removed from education and replaced by cultural motives to develop individuals, and improve society, the complex global challenges may begin to be tackled afresh.

The grand climate challenge

The most disturbing global challenge is climate crisis. I acknowledge that the notion of anthropogenic climate change is not universally agreed, and that while the science is clear the politics is not. There is a great deal of agreement among climate scientists that the planetary climate is changing in ways that increase risk for a large proportion of the global population. It is widely agreed that this is a result of a century of industrialized human lifestyle and that it is potentially irreversible. The most significant devastating effects on global human society in the foreseeable future are expected to be melting polar glaciers, leading to rising sea levels, flooding of Pacific islands, and inundation of low-lying countries and large coastal mega-cities. This is very likely to drive mass migration on a scale not seen for 10,000 years, but not many people are talking about this.

Because of the complexity of climate crisis all available pertinent knowledge needs to be brought together. I explore here whether parallels exist between the diverse approaches shown in my futures typology (see Table 1: Chapter 3) and current approaches to climate change (see Table 2).

The most common futures methods being used in climate research are trend analysis/modelling and expert scenario mapping based on the projections. These are heavily weighted towards the predictive/empirical approach and to a lesser degree towards the critical approach. Empirical and statistical data form the basis of expert, or top–down, scenarios used to evoke change. There may be value in collaboration between climate scientists and empirically oriented futures researchers. Collaboration would focus on the probable future as indicated by trend analysis and modelling. However, such approaches rarely elicit engagement or motivation from local communities, as they imply passive adaptation, rather than active participation.

The critical futures approach asks the question, 'who decides what is preferred?' This normative approach to climate futures is used in the UN Framework Convention on Climate Change (UNFCCC) agreement (1992), the Kyoto Protocol (1995), and the annual Conference of Parties (COPs). They critique existing climate insensitive activities associated with hyper-development. They also engage in collaboratively designed targets for reducing GreenHouse Gas (GHG) emissions to mitigate global warming, to enable preferred climate futures for the global population.

A climate approach based on the cultural/interpretive futures philosophy would critique the Western development model of hyper-development and neoliberal globalization taking a post-colonial or post-industrial view. It would evoke alternative possible climate futures by engaging with the voices of indigenous elders, women, youth, and hypothetical future generations.

Table 2 Futures approaches to climate change

Futures studies approaches	Futures studies key terms	Climate change approaches	Climate change key terms
Positivist approach: the future of climate change			
Predictive/ empirical	'probable future'	Climate trends 'Top–down Scenarios'	Trend is destiny Mitigation Passive adaptation
Pluralism of futures approaches to climate change			
Critical/ postmodern	'preferred futures'	UNFCCC protocols Emissions targets	2% Warmer stabilization
Cultural/ interpretive	'possible or alternative futures'	Women, youth, indigenous voices, Climate Alliances	Futures for the climate vulnerable
Participatory/ prospective	'prospective or participatory futures'	Climate activism 'Bottom–up' scenarios	Active co-evolution Social learning co-creation
Integral/ holistic	'planetary or integral futures'	UN protocols Global collaboration All of the above	Global climate justice

© 2009 Jennifer M. Gidley

Examples of climate protection aligned to this approach include the Climate Alliance of European Cities with the Indigenous Rainforest Peoples and the Australian Youth Climate Coalition.

The participatory futures approach involves informed forward thinking and active engagement to enable its empowering and transformative potential. While climate activism is participatory and action-oriented it needs to be well informed about the complexity of climate issues to claim wider legitimacy. Participatory futures involves community-based scenario building in climate-vulnerable communities and could be used worldwide to empower threatened communities. This approach could increase motivation towards household actions that can mitigate global warming, and also assist with the kind of social learning that supports adaptation.

Anthropogenic climate change is a planetary issue of meta-proportions and meta-complexity requiring global, national, regional, and local collaboration. An integral futures approach has much to offer climate futures in turning around current trends and finding creative ways to co-adapt to the inevitable. Although integral futures is not sufficiently embedded in either the futures field or the climate change field to have a large impact, the approach has potential for climate futures, particularly by integrating multiple approaches. Based on the expectation that sea levels will rise significantly in the foreseeable future, integrated approaches are being taken in low-lying countries like the Netherlands where architects are working with planners to create different kinds of floating houses and urban conurbations.

Conclusion

In this *Very Short Introduction* to the Future I have introduced you to multiple ways that we can think and talk about the future and shown its evolving relationship with time. Through a 3,000-year journey back in time I was able to give you a glimpse of the different ways that people have related to the future. The future has been prophesied, divined, imagined, colonized, feared, forecast, strategized, and created. As multifaceted as humanity itself the future can never be fully known, predicted, or controlled, but it can be better understood.

I have introduced you to the breadth and depth of the futures studies field, the range of approaches to exploring and creating multiple futures, and the extent of resources that can be tapped into. I have tried to offer some hope going forward by drawing on resources from my long-term engagement with futures studies, and sharing them with you. My working definition of futures studies is as follows:

> Futures Studies is the art and science of taking responsibility for the long-term consequences of our decisions and our actions today.

Once we know there is not one predictable future, as many leading-edge thinkers realized in the middle of the last century, we are freer to imagine alternative futures and work towards creating the futures we prefer—for self and humanity.

In my work over the years with young people, as a mother, an educator, a psychologist, and futurist, I found that young people are often very deeply affected by the negative images of the future portrayed in the media and dystopian movies. I learned that fear of the future or lack of ability to imagine a positive future can lead to depression, anxiety, and even suicide.

It is my hope that many young people will read this book. I want them to be aware of the grand global challenges faced by humanity, but not to be alarmed. A sense of fear and hopelessness often comes from not knowing enough. By introducing the challenges, hand in hand with the many alternatives and counter-trends, I want young people to feel inspired and empowered to change the trends they don't agree with. I want them to think creatively and imagine alternative futures that they could design.

By working collaboratively for positive change, whether in the area of climate change, alternative energy, humanitarian causes, health, economics, or transforming education, we can create a critical mass for creating positive futures.

We all have the capacity to create our desired futures, far more than most of us realize. As the only space where we have a degree of freedom, the future is a site of great power. Who holds that power in your life? The type of future we actually create reflects our values, ethics, morality, and level of consciousness.

I opened this *Very Short Introduction* to the Future with a provocative claim that the future we face is a threatening one. My intention was not to be a fear-monger but to raise awareness about the gravity of the challenges we do face. We can't change much from a place of ignorance: only from a place of awareness.

Although many of these challenges may seem insurmountable, they are in our power to deal with constructively if we choose to meet them with clarity, imagination, and courage. However, if we choose to keep our heads in the sand, and not care about our common human futures, we do so at our peril.

Appendix: Global futures timeline

1st MILLENNIUM BCE

1,000 >	The Sibyls.
1,000 >	The Prophets.
380	Plato *Republic*—utopian society based on justice.
145–90	Ssu-Ma Chien (Sīmǎ Qiān)—theory of cycles of virtue.
106–43	Cicero, Roman philosopher, distinction between 'facta' and 'futura'.
70–19	Virgil's *Fourth Eclogue*—images of Arcadia.

COMMON ERA

426	Augustine of Hippo *De civitate Dei* (*City of God*)—a utopian society.

12th century

c.1180	Joachim of Fiore—three great ages on earth, the third to begin 1260.

13th century

1260	Roger Bacon *Epistola de Secretis Operibus*—foresaw motor car, helicopter.

(continued)

14th century

1378   Ibn Khaldun *The Muqaddimah*—cyclical theory of social change.

15th century: The Italian Renaissance

*c.*1485   Da Vinci—flying machines and the *Ideal City*.

16th century

1516   More *Utopia*—community values stronger than individualism.

1543   Copernicus *On the Revolutions of the Heavenly Sphere*—new astronomy.

1555   Nostradamus *Les Propheties* (*The Prophecies*).

1589   De Molina *Concordia*—'futura' as contingent.

17th century: The scientific revolution

1602   Campanella *La città del sole* (*The City of the Sun*).

1627   Francis Bacon *The New Atlantis*—utopia of Enlightenment values.

1637   Descartes *Discourse on the Method*—Cartesian Rationalism.

1638   Godwin *The Man in the Moone*—first work of science fiction.

1662   Boyle's wishlist—twenty-four prophetic scientific predictions.

1686   de Fontenelle *Entretiens sur la pluralité des mondes*—life on other planets.

1687   Newton *Principia Mathematica*—birth of modern science.

1697   Leibniz *The Ultimate Origin of Things*—foreshadows Darwin's evolution.

18th century: The European Enlightenment

1748   La Mettrie *L'Homme machine* (*Man as Machine*).

1750	Turgot *A Philosophical Review of the Successive Advances of the Human Mind*.
1752	Maupertuis *Letters*—memory and 'prevision'.
1751–72	Diderot *Encyclopédie*—key text of French Enlightenment.
1760	Beginning of the Industrial Revolution in Britain.
1762	Rousseau *The Social Contract*—utopia of participatory democracy.
1765–83	The American Revolution—overthrew British, founded USA.
1771	Mercier *L'An 2440*—optimistic utopian novel.
1774	Herder *This Too a Philosophy of History for the Formation of Humanity*.
1781	Kant *Critique of Pure Reason*—key text of European Enlightenment.
1783	The launch of the Montgolfier balloon in Paris.
1786	The invention of the steam engine.
1789–99	The French Revolution.
1790s	The High Romantic period in Germany.
1795	de Condorcet *Outlines of an Historical View of the Progress of the Human Mind*.
1796	Goethe *Wilhelm Meister's Apprenticeship*—first *Bildungsroman*.
1798	Malthus *An Essay on the Principle of Population*.

19th century: The European Industrial Revolution

1800	Schelling *System of Transcendental Idealism*—conscious evolution.
1802	Restif de la Bretonne *Les Posthumes*—first fiction Superman.
1805	De Grainville *Le Dernier Homme* (*The Last Man*).
1818	Wollstonecraft Shelley *Frankenstein*.

(*continued*)

19th century: The European Industrial Revolution

1826	Wollstonecraft Shelley *The Last Man*.
1848	Marx and Engels *The Communist Manifesto*.
1859	Darwin *The Origin of Species*—theory of biological evolution.
1883–7	Nietzsche *Thus Spoke Zarathustra*—Übermensch (Superman)
1894	Steiner *The Philosophy of Freedom*—evolution of consciousness.
1895	Wells *The Time Machine*.

20th century

1901	Wells *Anticipations* and *The War of the Worlds*.
1907	Bergson *Creative Evolution*—alternative to Darwinian evolution.
1917	The October Revolution in Russia.
1922	Mumford *The Story of Utopias* and pioneering urban futures.
1927	Lang's movie *Metropolis*—first evil cinema robot.
1928	The USSR's first five-year plan.
1929	US President Hoover—Research Committee on Social Trends.
1930	Stapledon *Last and First Men*.
1932	Aldous Huxley *Brave New World*.
1929–39	Great Depression. Roosevelt's social engineering plan.
1939	New York World's Fair *The World of Tomorrow*.
1942	Asimov *The Three Laws of Robotics* in *Runaround*.
1944	Mumford *The Condition of Man*.
1945	Buckminster Fuller first Geodesic Dome.
1949	Flechtheim *Futurology: The New Science?* Orwell *1984*.

1950	Teilhard de Chardin *From the Pre-Human to the Ultra-Human*.
1955	Teilhard de Chardin *Le Phénomène humain* in French. Polak *The Image of the Future Volumes I & II*.
1956	Mumford *The Transformations of Man*.
1957	Berger founded Centre International de Prospective. Julian Huxley—first used term Transhumanism.
1959	Teilhard de Chardin *The Future of Man*. Galtung—Peace Research Institute, Oslo. Delphi method Helmer, Rescher, and Dalkey.
1960	De Jouvenel founded Association Internationale de Futuribles.
1960s	Kahn (RAND) *On Thermonuclear War*. Fuller *World Game*—players solve world problems.
1962	McLuhan *The Gutenberg Galaxy*—impact of Internet. Carson *The Silent Spring*—ecological awareness. Kahn *Thinking about the Unthinkable*. Aldous Huxley *Island*—utopian novel.
1964	De Jouvenel *L'Art de la conjecture*. McLuhan *Understanding Media*.
1965–73	*Commission on the Year 2000.*
1966	Ursula Le Guin *Rocannon's World*—her first futuristic novel. World Future Society—founded by Cornish.
1967	Mankind 2000: Conference Oslo, Norway.
1968	*Futures*—first futures journal founded UK. Club of Rome—founded by Peccei and King. *2001: A Space Odyssey* movie.
1969	Jungk and Galtung *Mankind 2000*: Proceedings. McHale *The Future of the Future*.

(*continued*)

20th century

1970	Özbekhan *The Predicament of Mankind* Club of Rome. Alvin and Heidi Toffler *Future Shock*.
1971	Hawai'i Research Center for Futures Studies—founded by Dator.
1972	Meadows with Randers *Limits to Growth*. Toffler (ed.) *The Futurists*.
1973	World Futures Studies Federation—founded Paris. Daniel Bell *Coming of Post-Industrial Society*.
1975	International University Centre, Dubrovnik. Fundación Javier Barros Sierra—founded Mexico.
1976	Kahn *The Next 200 Years*.
1977	Institute for Alternative Futures—founded by Bezold, Dator, Toffler. László *Goals for Mankind* to Club of Rome.
1979	*Mad Max*—early dystopian futures movie.
1982	Harman and Markley *Changing Images of Man*. Naisbitt *Megatrends*.
1983	Masini (ed.) *Visions of Desirable Societies*.
1986	International Futures Library, Salzburg—founded by Jungk. Drexler *Engines of Creation*—on nanotechnology.
1987	World Commission on Environment and Development.
1988	Hans Moravec *Mind Children*. Harman *Global Mind Change*.
1990	Barbara Adam *Time and Social Theory*. Elise Boulding *Building a Global Civic Culture*.
1990-6	UNESCO clearinghouse—Future Scan: FUTURESCO.

1993	Masini *Why Futures Studies?*
	Club of Budapest founded by László—human values, consciousness.
1997	Bell *The Foundations of Futures Studies Volumes I and II.*
	Slaughter *Knowledge Base of Futures Studies Volume I.*
1999	Morin *Homeland Earth: A Manifesto for the New Millennium.*
	The Matrix futures fiction movie.
2000	Inayatullah and Gidley (eds) *The University in Transformation.*
	Pieterse (ed.) *Global Futures: Shaping Globalization*

NB: See the main text for developments since 2000.

Sources: Janna Anderson (2006), *Futures Studies Timeline*; Jenny Andersson (2015), *Midwives of the Future*; Wendell Bell (1997), *Foundations of Futures Studies I*; I. F. Clarke (1979), *The Pattern of Expectation*; Johan Galtung and Sohail Inayatullah (1998), *Macrohistory and Macrohistorians*; Eleonora Masini (1982), *Reconceptualizing Futures*; and Wendy Schultz (2012), *The History of Futures*.

Appendix

References

Introduction

Warren W. Wagar (1983). H. G. Wells and the Genesis of Future Studies. *World Network of Religious Futurists*. Retrieved from <http://www.wnrf.org/cms/hgwells.shtml>.

Ossip K. Flechtheim (1949). Futurology: The New Science? *The Forum* (April), 206–9.

Bertrand de Jouvenel (1964/1967). *The Art of Conjecture* (translation of *L'Art de la conjecture* by Nikita Lary). London: Weidenfeld and Nicolson.

Lyman Tower Sargent (2010). *Utopianism: A Very Short Introduction*. Oxford: Oxford University Press.

Chapter 1: Three thousand years of futures

Jean Gebser (1949/1985). *The Ever-Present Origin*. Athens, Oh.: Ohio University Press.

Barbara Adam (2004). *Time (Key Concepts)*. Cambridge: Polity Press.

Eleonora Masini (1996). International Futures Perspectives and Cultural Concepts of the Future. In R. Slaughter (ed.), *The Knowledge Base of Futures Studies, Volume I*. Hawthorn, Victoria, Australia: DD Media Group.

Frederick L. Polak (1973). *The Image of the Future* (translated and abridged by Elise Boulding). San Francisco: Jossey-Bass.

Ignatius Frederick Clarke (1979). *The Pattern of Expectation: 1644–2001*. London: Jonathan Cape.

Tommaso Campanella (1901). *The City of the Sun*. In *Ideal Commonwealths*. New York: P. F. Collier & Son. Web edition published by eBooks@Adelaide.

Catherine Redford (2012). The Last Man. *Catherine Redford's Romanticism Blog*. <http://www.catherineredford.co.uk/2012/08/the-last-man.html>.

Chapter 2: The future multiplied

Jenny Andersson (2015). Midwives of the Future: Futurism, Futures Studies and the Shaping of the Global Imagination. In J. Andersson and E. Rindzeviciute (eds), *The Struggle for the Long-Term in Transnational Science and Politics: Forging the Future*: London: Routledge.

Nicholas Rescher (1998). *Predicting the Future: An Introduction to the Theory of Forecasting*. New York: SUNY Press.

Rolf Kreibich (2007). All Tomorrow's Crises. *IP—Global Edition* (Spring), 'Limits to Growth', 11–15.

Nicholas Rescher (1967). The Future as an Object of Research. RAND Corporation paper P-3593, Santa Monica, Calif.

Robert Jungk and Johan Galtung (eds) (1969). *Mankind 2000*. Oslo: George Allen & Unwin.

Chapter 3: The evolving scholarship of futures studies

James Dator (2009). Alternative Futures at the Manoa School. *Journal of Futures Studies*, 14(2), 1–18.

Johan Galtung (1982). *Schooling, Education and the Future* (Vol. 61). Malmo: Department of Education and Psychology Research, Lund University.

Jennifer M. Gidley (18–19 November 2010). Is Futures Studies Keeping up with the Times? Speculations on the Futures of Futures Thinking. Paper presented at the Stockholm Futures Conference 'Our Future in the Making', Stockholm.

Ziauddin Sardar (1999). *Rescuing All our Futures: The Future of Futures Studies*. Westport, Conn.: Praeger.

Elise Boulding (1988). Image and Action in Peace Building. *Journal of Social Issues*, 44(2), 17–37.

Richard Slaughter (2003). *Integral Futures: A New Model for Futures Enquiry and Practice*. Melbourne: Australian Foresight Institute.

Jennifer M. Gidley (2010). An Other View of Integral Futures: De/reconstructing the IF Brand. *Futures: The Journal of Policy, Planning and Futures Studies*, 42(2), 125–33.

Chapter 4: Crystal balls, flying cars, and robots

Braden R. Allenby and Daniel Searewitz (2011). *The Techno-Human Condition*. Boston: MIT Press.

Nick Bostrom (2014). *Superintelligence: Paths, Dangers and Strategies*. Oxford: Oxford University Press.

Verner Vinge (1993). The Coming Technological Singularity: How to Survive in the Post-Human Era. Paper presented at the VISION-21 Symposium.

Lewis Mumford (1946). *Values for Survival: Essays, Addresses, and Letters on Politics and Education*. New York: Harcourt Brace and Co.

Chapter 5: Technotopian or human-centred futures?

Oliver Markley and Willis Harman (1982). *Changing Images of Man*. Oxford: Pergamon Press.

Chad Wellmon (2011). Touching Books: Diderot, Novalis, and the Encyclopedia of the Future. *Representations*, 114 (Spring), 65–102.

Alison Bashford (2013). Julian Huxley's Transhumanism. In M. Turda (ed.), *Crafting Humans: From Genesis to Eugenics and Beyond*. Taiwan: V & R Unipress National Taiwan University Press.

Michael Murphy (1992). *The Future of the Body: Explorations into the Further Evolution of Human Nature*. Los Angeles: Jeremy P. Tarcher.

Jennifer M. Gidley (2010). Globally Scanning for Megatrends of the Mind: Potential Futures of 'Futures Thinking'. *Futures: The Journal of Policy, Planning and Futures Studies*, 42(10), 1040–8.

Duane Elgin and Coleen LeDrew (1997). *Global Consciousness Change: Indicators of an Emerging Paradigm*, San Anselmo, Calif.: The Millennium Project.

Chapter 6: Grand global futures challenges

James Dator (2009). The Unholy Trinity, Plus One. *Journal of Futures Studies*, 13(3), 33–48.

Jorgen Randers (2012). *A Global Forecast for the Next 40 Years: 2052.* White River Junction, Vt: Chelsea Green Publishing.

Hazel Henderson (2014). *Mapping the Global Transition to the Solar Age: From 'Economism' to Earth System Science.* London: ICAEW.

Maurizio Carta (2007). *Creative City: Dynamics, Innovations, Actions.* Barcelona: LISt Laboratorio.

Jennifer M. Gidley (2016). Understanding the Breadth of Futures Studies through a Dialogue with Climate Change. *World Future Review*, 8(1), 24–38.

Further reading and websites

General books

Here is a brief selection of classic futures books. See also
<http://www.wfsf.org/resources/futures-publications-books>.

Adam, B., and Groves, C. (2007). *Future Matters: Action, Knowledge, Ethics (Supplements to the Study of Time)*. Leiden: Brill.

Bell, W. (1997). *Foundations of Futures Studies I & II*. New Brunswick, NJ: Transaction Publishers.

Binde, J. (2001) (ed.) *Keys to the 21st Century*. Paris: UNESCO & Berghahn Books.

de Jouvenel, B. (1964/1967). *The Art of Conjecture* (translation of *L'Art de la Conjecture* by Nikita Lary). London: Weidenfeld and Nicolson.

Gidley, J., and Inayatullah, S. (2002). *Youth Futures: Comparative Research and Transformative Visions*. Westport, Conn.: Praeger.

Inayatullah, S., and Gidley, J. (eds) (2000). *The University in Transformation: Global Perspectives on the Futures of the University*. Westport, Conn.: Bergin & Garvey.

Jungk, R., and Galtung, J. (eds) (1969). *Mankind 2000*. Oslo: George Allen & Unwin.

Masini, E. (1993). *Why Future Studies?* London: Grey Seal.

Slaughter, R. (1999). *Futures for the Third Millennium: Enabling the Forward View*. St Leonards, NSW: Prospect Media.

Journals

As the academic field of futures studies developed several academic journals were founded.

Here is a brief selection of peer reviewed futures and foresight journals with URLs. See also:

<http://www.wfsf.org/resources/futures-publications-journals>.

Futures: The Journal of Policy, Planning and Futures Studies, London: Elsevier, founded 1969.

<http://www.journals.elsevier.com/futures/>.

European Journal of Futures Research, Berlin: Springer, founded 2013. <http://www.springer.com/philosophy/history+of+science/journal/40309>.

Futuribles, Paris: Futuribles International, founded 1960. <https://www.futuribles.com/en/>.

World Future Review, Hawai'i: Sage, founded 2009. <https://au.sagepub.com/en-gb/oce/world-future-review/journal202156#description>.

Foresight: The Journal of Future Studies, Strategic Thinking and Policy, London: Emerald, founded 1999.

<http://www.emeraldgrouppublishing.com/products/journals/journals.htm?PHPSESSID=if4gij4mdfomo157e0oprpafj1&id=fs>.

Web resources

Here are links to a handful of key players on the global stage.

World Futures Studies Federation: <www.wfsf.org>.

Association of Professional Futurists: <apf.org>.

The Future of Humanity Institute: <www.fhi.ox.ac.uk>.

World Future Council: <www.worldfuturecouncil.org>.

World Future Society: <www.wfs.org>.

The Millennium Project: <www.millennium-project.org>.

Introduction

Good overviews on naming the study of the future are Wendell Bell (1996), An Overview of Futures Studies. In R. Slaughter (ed.), *The Knowledge Base of Futures Studies, Volume I*. Hawthorn, Victoria, Australia: DD Media Group; Eleonora Masini (1993), *Why Future Studies?* London: Grey Seal; Ziauddin Sardar (2010), The Namesake: Futures; Futures Studies; Futurology; Futuristic; Foresight—What's in a Name? *Futures: The Journal of Policy, Planning and Futures Studies*, 42(3), 177–84.

A good overview on time and the future is Barbara Adam (2004), *Time (Key Concepts)*. Cambridge: Polity Press.

Of historical interest is H. G. Wells (1932/1987), 'Wanted Professors of Foresight!' *Futures Research Quarterly (World Future Society)* (Spring).

Chapter 1: Three thousand years of futures

For an overview of evolution of consciousness theories in relation to time consciousness see Jennifer M. Gidley (2007), The Evolution of Consciousness as a Planetary Imperative: An Integration of Integral Views. *Integral Review: A Transdisciplinary and Transcultural Journal for New Thought, Research and Praxis*, 5, 4–226; Ken Wilber (1981/1996), *Up from Eden*. Wheaton, Ill.: Quest Books.

A good overview of macrohistory is Johan Galtung and Sohail Inayatullah (1998), *Macrohistory and Macrohistorians*. Westport, Conn.: Praeger.

The best overview on the broad history of futures thinking is Wendell Bell (1997/2003), *Foundations of Futures Studies I: History, Purposes, Knowledge*. New Brunswick, NJ: Transaction Publishers. For a short history of futures studies see Wendy Schultz (2012), The History of Futures. In A. Curry (ed.), *The Future of Futures* (pp. 3–7): Association of Professional Futurists.

Overviews of utopias and dystopias are Lyman Tower Sargent (2010), *Utopianism: A Very Short Introduction*. Oxford: Oxford University Press; and Gregory Claeys (ed.) (2010), *The Cambridge Companion to Utopian Literature*. Cambridge: Cambridge University Press.

Chapter 2: The future multiplied

Overview of the pluralism shift in philosophy: Jürgen Habermas (1972), *Knowledge and Human Interests* (2nd edn). London: Heinemann.

For histories of futures thinking in the Cold War period, see Jenny Andersson (2012), The Great Future Debate and the Struggle for the World. *American Historical Review*, 117(5), 1411–30; Elke Seefried (2014), Steering the Future: The Emergence of 'Western' Futures Research and its Production of Expertise, 1950s to early 1970s. *European Journal of Futures Research*, 2(1), 1–12; Hyeonju Son (2015), The History of Western Futures Studies: An Exploration of the Intellectual Traditions and Three-Phase Periodization. *Futures: The Journal of Policy, Planning and*

Futures Studies, 66, 120–37; and a special issue of *Futures* (2005) Volume 37, No. 5.

An overview of personal futures approach is Verne Wheelwright (2012), *It's your Future…Make it a Good One!* Harlingen, Tex.: Personal Futures Network.

Chapter 3: The evolving scholarship of futures studies

Other typologies of futures approaches include: Sohail Inayatullah (1990), Deconstructing and Reconstructing the Future: Predictive, Cultural and Critical Epistemologies. *Futures*, 22(2), 115–41; Richard Slaughter (1999), Professional Standards in Futures Work. *Futures: The Journal of Policy, Planning and Futures Studies*, 31(8), 835–51; Peter Moll (1996), The Thirst for Certainty: Futures Studies in Europe and the United States. In R. Slaughter (ed.), *The Knowledge Base of Futures Studies, Volume 1*. Melbourne, Victoria: Foresight International; and Éva Hideg (2015), *Paradigms in Futures Field, Volume 21*. Budapest: Corvinus University.

For wider reading on advancing futures concepts see Eleonora Masini (1982), Reconceptualizing Futures: A Need and a Hope. *World Future Society Bulletin* (November–December), 1–8; and Richard Slaughter (1999), *Futures for the Third Millennium: Enabling the Forward View*. St Leonards, NSW: Prospect Media.

To explore the integral futures controversy see special issues of *Futures* (2008) Volume 40(2); *Futures* (2010) Volume 42(2); and special issue of *Journal of Integral Theory and Practice*, 6(2).

Extended concepts of time can be explored in Elise Boulding (1990), *Building a Global Civic Culture: Education for an Interdependent World*. New York: Syracuse University Press; Danny Hillis, Rob Seaman, Steve Allen, and Jon Giorgini (2012), *Time in the 10,000-Year Clock*. Washington, DC: American Astronomical Society.

Good overviews of futures methods are found in Richard A. Slaughter with Marcus Bussey (2005/2012), *Futures Thinking for Social Foresight*. Brisbane: Foresight International; Joseph Voros (2003), A Generic Foresight Process Framework. *Foresight*, 5(3), 20–1; Michael Jackson (2013), *Practical Foresight Guide—Shaping Tomorrow*, chapter 3 <https://www.shapingtomorrow.com/media-centre/pf-ch03.pdf>; Jerome C. Glenn and Theodore J. Gordon (2009), *Futures Research Methodology Version 3.0*, The Millennium Project.

Chapter 4: Crystal balls, flying cars, and robots

Best overviews of contemporary transhumanism and posthumanism are Nick Bostrom (2003/5), Transhumanist Values. In F. Adams (ed.), *Ethical Issues for the 21st Century*. Oxford: Philosophical Documentation Centre Press; Nick Bostrom (2008), Why I Want to be a Posthuman When I Grow up. In B. Gordijn and R. Chadwick (eds), *Medical Enhancement and Posthumanity* (107–37). New York: Springer.

For an overview of Kurzweil's singularity theory see Ray Kurzweil (2006), *The Singularity is Near: When Humans Transcend Biology*. New York: Penguin; The Viking Press.

Neo-Cornucopian approaches include Byron Reese (2013), *Infinite Progress: How the Internet and Technology will End Ignorance, Disease, Poverty, Hunger and War*. Austin, Tex.: Greenleaf Books.

Neo-Malthusian approaches include Lindsay Grant (1993), Cornucopian Fallacies. *Focus*, 3(2); Jared Diamond (2005), *Collapse: How Societies Choose to Fail or Succeed*. New York: Viking.

For discussion on existential risk related to AI see Nick Bostrom (2014), *Superintelligence: Paths, Dangers and Strategies*. Oxford: Oxford University Press; Jaron Lanier (2013), *Who Owns the Future?* New York: Simon & Schuster.

Chapter 5: Technotopian or human-centred futures?

For more on human-centred images see Fred Polak (1973), *The Image of the Future* (translated and abridged by Elise Boulding). San Francisco: Jossey-Bass; Jacques Attali (2006/2009), *A Brief History of the Future: A Brave and Controversial Look at the Twenty-First Century* (translated by J. Leggatt). New York: Skyhorse Publishing.

Origins of humanistic transhumanism: see Pierre Teilhard de Chardin (1959/2002), *The Phenomenon of Man*. New York: Perennial; Pierre Teilhard de Chardin (1959/2004), *The Future of Man*. New York: Image Books, Doubleday; Julian Huxley (1957), Transhumanism. In J. Huxley (ed.), *New Bottles for New Wine* (pp. 13–17). London: Chatto & Windus.

Further reading on naturally evolving superhuman theories includes Henri Bergson (1907/1944), *Creative Evolution* (translated by A. Mitchell). New York: Macmillan & Co.; Rudolf Steiner

(1914/1973), *The Riddles of Philosophy (GA 18)* (4th edn). Spring Valley, NY: The Anthroposophic Press; Michael Murphy (1992), *The Future of the Body: Explorations into the Further Evolution of Human Nature.* Los Angeles: Jeremy P. Tarcher.

Overviews of evolution of consciousness and human-centred futures include Abraham Maslow (1971), *The Farther Reaches of Human Nature.* New York: The Viking Press; Ken Wilber (2000), *Integral Psychology: Consciousness, Spirit, Psychology, Therapy.* Boston: Shambhala; and Ervin László (2006), *The Chaos Point: The World at the Crossroads.* Charlottsville, Va: Hampton Roads Publishing Company, Inc.

Good overviews on cultural evolution are Richard Tarnas (1991), *The Passions of the Western Mind.* New York: Random House; Jürgen Habermas (1979), *Communication and the Evolution of Society.* Boston: Beacon Press.

Good overviews on postformal reasoning are Jan Sinnot (1998), *The Development of Logic in Adulthood: Postformal Thought and its Applications.* New York: Springer; Michael L. Commons and Sara Ross (2008), What Postformal Thought is, and Why it Matters. *World Futures,* 64, 321–9; and Jennifer M. Gidley (2016), 'Postformal in Psychology' (chapter 5) in *Postformal Education: A Philosophy for Complex Futures.* Dordrecht: Springer.

Chapter 6: Grand global futures challenges

Overviews on the global challenges: see World Economic Forum *Outlook on the Global Agenda Report 2015*; and Jerome C. Glenn, Elizabeth Florescu, and The Millennium Project Team 2015–2016 State of the Future Report.

Good reading on the new urbanization including creative cities: see Tigran Haas (ed.) (2008), *New Urbanism and Beyond: Designing Cities for the Future.* New York: Rizzoli; Sasha Kagan (2010), Workshop 3: Sustainable Creative Cities: The Role of the Arts in Globalised Urban Contexts. In *4th Connecting Civil Societies in Asia and Europe (CCS4) Conference.* Brussels: Leuphana, Institut für Kulturtheorie.

Introductions to the post-industrial creative culture include Paul Ray (1996), The Rise of Integral Culture. *Noetic Sciences Review,* 37, Spring; Richard Florida (2002), *The Rise of the Creative Class; and How It's Transforming Work, Leisure, Community and Everyday Life.* New York: Basic Books.

For an overview on educational challenges and transformation see
Jennifer M. Gidley (2016), *Postformal Education: A Philosophy for Complex Futures*. Dordrecht: Springer International; and Edgar Morin (2001), *Seven Complex Lessons in Education for the Future*. Paris: UNESCO.

Further reading on the climate crisis and approaches to it: see
Intergovernmental Panel on Climate Change (IPCC), *IPCC, 2014*: R. K. Pachauri and L. A. Meyer (2014) (eds), *Climate Change 2014: Synthesis Report. Contribution of Working Groups I, II and III to the Fifth Assessment Report of the Intergovernmental Panel on Climate Change*. Geneva: IPCC.

Index

The Future

AFRICAN HISTORY
A Very Short Introduction
John Parker & Richard Rathbone

Essential reading for anyone interested in the African continent
and the diversity of human history, this *Very Short Introduction*
looks at Africa's past and reflects on the changing ways it has
been imagined and represented. Key themes in current thinking
about Africa's history are illustrated with a range of fascinating
historical examples, drawn from over 5 millennia across this
vast continent.

'A very well informed and sharply stated historiography...should
be in every historiography student's kitbag. A tour de force...it
made me think a great deal.'

Terence Ranger,
The Bulletin of the School of Oriental and African Studies

BEAUTY
A Very Short Introduction
Roger Scruton

In this *Very Short Introduction* the renowned philosopher Roger Scruton explores the concept of beauty, asking what makes an object - either in art, in nature, or the human form - beautiful, and examining how we can compare differing judgements of beauty when it is evident all around us that our tastes vary so widely. Is there a right judgement to be made about beauty? Is it right to say there is more beauty in a classical temple than a concrete office block, more in a Rembrandt than in last year's Turner Prize winner? Forthright and thought-provoking, and as accessible as it is intellectually rigorous, this introduction to the philosophy of beauty draws conclusions that some may find controversial, but, as Scruton shows, help us to find greater sense of meaning in the beautiful objects that fill our lives.

A fascinating book, which I heartily recommend.

Brya Wilson, Readers Digest

www.oup.com/vsi